DEAD WOOD

Engaging the Disengaged in Today's Right-Sized Workplace

Robert M. Khoury, Ph.D.

☯

How to survive, outwit, and make the most of your organization's underachieving screwups, sacred cows, ass-kissers, laurel-resters, heinie-coverers and all-around bad apples, and turn to your advantage the numbest of skulls because they are untouchable, they can't be fired, and you are stuck with them.

The top ten winning commandments plus 25 laser-guided survival norms of managing and working with those underperforming, good-for-nothing but secure, hard-to-get-rid-of slackers, goof-offs, and nitwits who fill a much-needed void in your company and give the word unproductive a bad name. Transform Corporate America's useless Dead Wood into useful Fire Wood to fuel organizational success in a right-sized working world where every employee, even failures count.

ISBN: 1-4196-7584-2
ISBN-13: 978-1419675843
Library of Congress Control Number: 2007909907

Visit www.booksurge.com to order additional copies.

Flip the author a message at rmkhoury@earthlink.net.

Front cover photo courtesy of pdphoto.org.
Back cover USDA photo courtesy of geekphilosopher.com.

For JOAN, my wife, who worked with these annoying people everyday, but whose wisdom and courage inspired me to care about them.

Content:

Survival Norms:

Introduction:

Have you ever worked with someone who is always busy and appears to be hard working, but in the end all that activity never seems to produce any meaningful results or add anything of value? Have you ever supervised an employee who is always the first one to volunteer for any new assignment, and insists on being involved with everything, but never seems to contribute anything more useful than to show up on time? Have you ever worked for a boss whose concept of leadership consists entirely of handing out work and delegating assignments, preferably his own? Do you feel surrounded by empty figureheads who are always arriving late and leaving early, and in between, spend all of their time using stupid cunning to spin fantastic lies that their secretaries then use to con(vince) you that they need to arrive late and leave early? Do you daydream about getting rid of the weeds in your corporate garden so the flowers can grow? Are you at the end of your rope? Well, maybe it's time, as the saying goes, to tie a knot.

One:
Why me, God?

You are most definitely not alone. It's the worst kind of rumor that only 15 to 20% of employees produce 80% of their company's value … a true rumor. And the negative behavior of the many is more damaging than the positive behavior of the few is healing. In other words, one bad apple can spoil the whole barrel, but one or two good performers cannot unspoil it.

Corporate America worries too much about recruiting talent and raiding talent, and ought to be worrying a lot more about the massive waste of talent already in its ranks. Companies are filled with talented employees who feel alienated, underemployed, meaningless, powerless, and estranged, who are simply coasting toward oblivion with full pay and health benefits. The numbers will impress you as much as hard, bitter experience has depressed you. In 2007, the Gallup Organization, as quoted in the "Wall Street Journal," reported that 70% of all U.S. employees say they feel either "not engaged" or "actively disengaged" at work, and that companies with high numbers of disengaged workers have higher absenteeism, lower productivity, and higher turnover. Duh.

Survival Norm #1: Start Fresh!
People say that if you forget the past, then you are bound to repeat it. But I say to you that by concentrating on the past, and dwelling on it, you are liable to ignore the only true reality, the here and now, which has the potential to

answer all your questions and solve your problems. Up to now, you have made mistakes, lots of them, in managing your working relationship with Dead Wood. You tried to correct his shortcomings, but everything you did turned out badly and you failed completely. Worse, in the process, you became painfully aware of your own limitations, weaknesses, and deficiencies. You have many regrets about the past and many more fears about the future. Now is the time to free yourself of all those mistakes, regrets, and shortcomings, and give yourself a fresh start! Only by shedding the past and cleansing yourself of your disappointments and fears, like a snake that casts off its skin, can you make room for right thoughts and right actions to come. It's a ritual dating back hundreds of years, because it works. Write down on a piece of paper your past mistakes, failures, disappointments, shortcomings, and whatever else has blocked you from achieving success with Dead Wood. Concentrate on what you are doing. Visualize your mistakes and regrets. Imagine the relief you will feel when your problems are resolved. Then set the paper on fire. Watch carefully as it burns. Lighting the paper symbolizes a transition and a cleansing. As the flaming paper disappears, you will experience a profound feeling of liberation and release and, finally, peace. Your mistakes and failings have disappeared, as if they never existed. Then take another piece of paper. Write a letter to yourself, a treasure map. Write about your mission to rehabilitate Dead Wood for the next 12 months.

Write down in detail how you are going to engage the disengaged, turn the worthless into the worthwhile and the useless into the useful. Be specific. Start by defining your goals and aspirations, projecting where you want to be in a year. Next, define the steps you need to take each month throughout the year to get there. Concentrate. Visualize. Seal the letter in an envelope. Address the envelope to yourself. Ask a friend to mail it to you in one year. Right thoughts equal right actions. Jesus said that lusting is the same as adultery. That means thought is the same as action. Documenting your goals and mapping out your plans and aspirations will make them come true. On the other hand, if you don't know where you're going, you can't get there from here.

The truth is that every company, every work organization, and every bureaucracy has its vulnerable underbelly of Dead Wood, those employees who fill a much-needed void in the working world by never failing to underachieve or disappoint. In companies small and large, growing and shrinking, in every sector under the sun, in every rank in the hierarchy of authority, and in every job title up to and including the top positions in the organization, there is Dead Wood. In 2006, in an online survey, Staffing.org, a research firm, asked 300 people to describe their company's workforce using fictional places. About 80% said it is a lot like "The Office" or "Dilbert". And what about your CEO, who refers proudly to you and your colleagues as "The (Your company name here) Family"? Only 5% reported that it is more like the Cleaver's on "Leave It to Beaver".

The good news is that every rational organization can tolerate a certain amount of irrational Dead Wood and even learn to use it productively. The bad news is that too much brain-dead Dead Wood will eventually undermine the organization's success and jeopardize its very survival.

(I have a large workshop to share, consisting of many practical tools and techniques that not only will reveal a clear understanding of unproductive underachievers, but also will show you how to use Dead Wood as a means of bettering oneself and one's work environment. And because I want my advice to be easy to identify and digest, the way forward is filled with Survival Norms, steppingstones used in crossing shark-infested waters on your journey to The Ten Commandments on the other side. Now "the way" could be a deeply profound metaphor for Enlightenment or Inner Peace, or it could represent nothing more than the next 12 chapters, if you know what I mean. You must be the judge of that.)

Survival Norm #2: Be Here Now!

Job prospecting used to be so simple and straightforward. Fatter paycheck, fancier title, bigger turf, and it was goodbye to "There is no 'I' in T-E-A-M" and hello, "Greed is good!" Goodbye Ford Focus, Hello BMW 3 Series! Goodbye Housewife, Hello Trophy Wife! Now, it's about more than company loyalty versus personal ambition. Now, it's all about the trade-offs. The extra cash and corner office are nice. And your new company has some bright, caring people who appreciate, respect, and work well with people like you. But now you've discovered that many more of your new bosses and teammates are fools, jerks, and airheads, and that they are more secure than you want them to be. You hit yourself on the head with the organizational chart and heard a loud, hollow sound, and now you realize that it doesn't mean your head is empty. Job hopping used to be so simple. You didn't wind up wondering, "Am I better off now, or what?" True, it's always been wise to look before you leap. The difference today, cubicle warrior, is that you need a thermometer, a hot water bottle, a parachute, and a microscope to protect and defend yourself.

When a board of directors loses faith in its CEO, what are the board members usually so angry about? A highly respected 2005 study, reported in "Business Week," quizzed over 1,000 directors about what caused them to fire their CEOs. Among the top three reasons: Over one-quarter were dismissed because they "tolerated low performers." The moral of the study is pretty clear: "Managers who do not manage Dead Wood deserve to be treated like Dead Wood."

You picked up this little book and are halfheartedly reading it right now because in your working life today, you cannot avoid working with Dead Wood, it's causing big problems, and you need to know what you can do about it. Up to now, you have tried everything you can think of without success and are feeling angry and frustrated at the injustice of it all. You even tried ignoring the problem and turning a blind eye to the Dead Wood. But you discovered that the hidden cost of compromising your high standards and expectations is your own self-respect and commitment to professionalism, and now you feel even worse. You have reached the conclusion that your situation is probably hopeless and are therefore more than a little skeptical that some over-credentialed egghead like me can really help you deal with co-workers who are "dead on the vine."

Well, be not unbelieving, but believing. If you think Corporate America is replete with Dead Wood, you're right, but the Ivory Tower is worse. Because of lifetime job security, union power, and collective bargaining contracts that impose hundreds of protective bureaucratic work rules, removing ineffective teachers from the classroom is still virtually impossible. Even though this nation has invested trillions of dollars trying to improve public schooling for decades, our children cannot compete and are becoming unemployable in the 21st Century, globalized workplace.

Depending on your level of frustration, or perhaps your blood-alcohol level, it may give you some satisfaction to learn that Dead Wood is a daily challenge for almost everyone everywhere in the working world today.

General Motors, the venerated auto company, has mastered only half the solution for a company that finds itself overstaffed with Dead Wood. GM has managed to get rid of the job while keeping the jobholder on the payroll. The "Wall Street Journal" reported in 2005 that according to the "Detroit Free Press," enrolled in GM's so-called "Jobs Bank" were 3,500 union members each collecting wages and benefits of about $100,000 a year for doing nothing, at an annual cost to the company of $350 million. And that's just the tip of the iceberg according to a WSJ follow-up story in 2006. The Jobs Bank at GM and all other U.S. auto companies including Ford cost around $2 billion that year to pay about 15,000 auto workers after their companies stop needing them. Their "job" at the Jobs Bank: To Do Nothing. Dead Wood may have more than a little to do with why Detroit is facing bankruptcy while Japanese auto makers grow and prosper.

Why is the United Nations so insusceptible to effective reform? The main reason is that its 18,000 bureaucrats are hired according to region and nationality, not merit. The 2005 reform effort included a one-time buyout of nonperforming officials. But unless merit becomes the basis for hiring from now on, new Dead Wood will replace the old Dead Wood.

At the end of 2006, Intel, the giant chip maker, admitting that its management structure had become bloated with Dead Wood, announced that it is laying off 1,000 managers to improve efficiency. Intel said that the cuts would affect all levels of management and all geographies, and also hinted at more cutting down the road.

Dead Wood is a stubborn fact of working life to be acknowledged by all bureaucracies. Moreover, Dead Wood has become one of the defining, essential characteristics of post-modern work organizations everywhere, even across oceans and cultures. The giant state-owned French power utility known as EDF has at any given time as many as 5,000 executives who are without a job description or a real work assignment. In a 2005 "Wall Street Journal" article, current and former employees including the previous co-COO reported that these executives, who come to work every day without anything to do, each have an office and a secretary and spend all of their time in bogus, make-work meetings.

You can throw a brick out of the window of America's corporate headquarters and hit a company where the French solution is in play. "Put him in a cupboard (or cubicle) and throw away the key," as the French saying goes. Push your Dead Wood out of the way, marginalize them, ignore them, leave them with nothing to do, and hope that they will eventually do the right thing and quit with the usual face-saving fib – "Because I need to spend more time with my family." It is a strategy with a considerable pricetag for the company. For one thing, it's expensive financially. Dead Wood will continue to draw a salary as long as he shows up for work most of the time ("Working From Home" counts), doesn't cause anyone any trouble, and doesn't do a bad, bad thing. For Dead Wood's workmates, it's "expensive" emotionally and even spiritually, as you have probably learned from bitter experience, and we will discuss.

The bottom line is simply this: In today's right-sized workplace, there is probably more money to be made from turning useless Dead Wood into productive Fire Wood than from most anything else Corporate America has up its sleeve. There is less to fear from outside competition than from inside Dead Wood.

Management textbooks written by academics that have never left the Ivory Tower, and overbearing, self-important testimonials on leadership authored by football coaches, talkshow hosts, and any one of the Kennedys will not help you much. That's because, never-been-there/never-done-that/never-bought-the-T-shirt aside, many of our most esteemed publications and brand-name cultural commissars consistently blame managers and corporate leaders for their Dead Wood. If you were a more inspiring leader, these management gurus preach, and for $29.95 (hardcover), you too can be, then you would have no trouble turning useless Dead Wood into productive Fire Wood. Leadership precedes Followership. Let's focus on finding out what's wrong with you and fixing it. Whoa! What's wrong with *you*? Why can't *you* rise to the challenge!? The real problem, they say, is not Dead Wood, but your personal inadequacy and sorry lack of leadership ability. (As if to deny the indisputable fact that any kind of leadership requires some shred of followership, hopelessly devoid of that which makes Dead Wood Dead Wood in the first place.)

Holy cow! Talk about blaming the victim.

The rest subscribe to the Pyramid Assumption. That's the argument that the more Dead Wood it has, the better for the organization it is, because to produce a little Fire Wood (at the top of the pyramid) requires a lot of Dead Wood (at the bottom).

Now that's eyeroll-worthy.

Survival Norm #3: Reason and Shame Don't Work!

Management gurus don't waste their time and attention on underperformers, and simply ignore them, assuming that they can always be persuaded to leave, and eventually do let go. When an employee has been languishing in the bottom 10% for a sustained period of time, the manager can just start a conversation about moving on and it will happen naturally. Once in a blue moon, the underperformer doesn't want to go. But if the manager explains how the organization sees him, and uses precise geometric logic to show how much better off he will be in another company where his skills are a better fit, then most people will bow to reason and can be shamed into leaving without making a fuss. Yeah, right! Start making sense! First, people doing hard work, adding value, and earning their paycheck resist being let go. How much more will Dead Wood fight to keep his free ride on the gravy train? Which one sounds more illogical? Giving up a good job without a fight, or, giving up a better job without a fight? Second, every payday underperformers are shame-fighting, by cashing checks that they know they don't deserve. After a sustained period of time, Dead Wood will have no shame left to leverage. Long story short: To drive away Dead Wood, reason is a stumbling block and shame has no sting.

Seeing things as they are, making sense of Dead Wood, and using the take-aways I will teach you to more effectively deal with underachievers, will add tranquility to your working life and help restore order to your working world. Otherwise, there's always medicinal marijuana.

Two:
What is Dead Wood, exactly?

Dead Wood is easier to recognize than to define. Dead Wood is one of those primitive notions that are difficult to express because it is one of our deepest feelings about the way some people are and the way they behave at work. Judged on activity rather than results, Dead Wood is busy, but never productive. Dead Wood is involved, but never engaged. Dead Wood facilitates, but never helps. Dead Wood leads by being behind you every step of the way. Dead Wood's clothes look dirty, but his hands are always clean.

This may sound contrary to common sense at first, but basically, Dead Wood is any employee whose job performance is not quite satisfactory and not quite unsatisfactory.

Say what?

(Fire Wood is a residual category, consisting of engaged, productive workers like you and your peers who are not Dead Wood. Furthermore, let's agree that words of any gender used herein will include any other gender, and in no way limit its scope or intent, but are used only as a matter of convenience. In other words, Dead Wood is an asexual and gender-nonspecific term.)

Huh?

Dead Wood is what?

Let me briefly explain.

Popular culture regards job performance as a dichotomy or as divided into two and only two kinds. That is to say, a worker's performance on this or that assignment will be judged either satisfactory or unsatisfactory, and overall, a worker's total performance on all assignments and responsibilities also must be one or the other, good or bad, but cannot be both.

However, to be more precise, job performance should not be seen as a black-and-white, either/or proposition, but as a continuum or scale having two ideal types, Satisfactory and Unsatisfactory, one at each end, where one's real-life job performance falls somewhere in between these two abstract extremes. In the real-life world of work, there is no bright line between the satisfactory and the unsatisfactory. It may give you a great deal of emotional and even spiritual contentment to make believe that every worker must be either satisfactory or unsatisfactory, productive or nonproductive, success or failure. It may help you uncomplicate the complicated and make sense of your working world. But it will also keep you from better understanding and making the most of Dead Wood.

Therefore, consider the middle way on our job performance scale. (Apologies to the Buddha.) What does it mean? If one's job performance is judged not quite satisfactory enough to justify keeping the employee on the payroll for the work he does, but at the same time, is judged not quite unsatisfactory enough to justify separating the employee from the organization for doing the work so poorly that it almost wasn't worth doing in the first place, then he is Dead Wood – not altogether one nor altogether the other.

Okay, so the "whatness" of Dead Wood put into words is a brain-full. Fear not. You will see it when you know it. For the time being, take your choice: Dead

Wood is a successful failure or a failed success that you are stuck with and can't fire.

Survival Norm #4: The Holey Parable of Dead Wood and Fire Wood

Once upon a time Dead Wood and Fire Wood and a couple of their workmates were ordered by their boss to dig a big hole in the ground. They gathered picks and shovels and hiked down the road to where they had been told to dig. Now this was during the hot summer season, and they had a long walk to get there. So by the time they arrived, they were already dead-tired. Nevertheless, being good workers, they started digging. The hole was seven feet deep when Fire Wood looked up and realized that Dead Wood was not digging with them. He climbed out of the hole, and found Dead Wood sound asleep under a nearby tree. Fire Wood burst into anger, "Why should you rest while we work? Do you think you are better than the rest of us that you should do as you please while we follow orders?" Standing, Dead Wood calmly reached out, and rested his hand on the tree. "Pick up your shovel, Fire Wood. I want you to hit my hand with it as hard as you can." Fire Wood swung his shovel like Babe Ruth on steroids! But Dead Wood jerked his hand away at the last moment, and Fire Wood struck the tree with all his might! When he had stopped shaking, Fire Wood pulled himself together and climbed back into the hole. "Why isn't Dead Wood helping us dig?" asked his teammates. "I'll show you why," he replied. Fire Wood placed his hand over his face. "Pick up your shovel ..."

To be right is not enough. You have to be cleverer. Verily, I say to you, if you listen to my teachings, and do not waver, but practice the things that I say, Dead Wood's testicles will soon be hanging like fuzzy dice from the rearview mirror of your car.

Three:
Fit happens:

How does an organization accumulate Dead Wood?

How much Dead Wood does the average organization have?

How much Dead Wood is considered too much Dead Wood?

The ultimate goal of every work organization in talent management of its human labor is one and the same: To recruit, motivate, and retain the right person in the right job. Dead Wood is generally the result of "poor fit," which is to say, of employing the wrong person in the right job. For the wrong person in the right job will inevitably make the right job wrong, just as the right person in the wrong job will make the wrong job right.

Survival Norm #5: Flee or Pee?

There is one and only one defining characteristic of the post-modern zeitgeist that PC nazis all agree on: Yesterday, standards were falling. Today, they are fading away. Nowhere is this more obvious than in the world of work. As workplaces have become more tolerant and more accepting of individual tastes and preferences, behavior has become weirder and weirder. Managers and co-workers are faced with deciding where to draw the line. When do you accommodate or even ignore Dead Wood and when is it time to take action? You can't pick a fight with every weirdo, but you don't want to run away from one either. Flee or Pee? First, decide on your bottom line. You want your business and office to function smoothly. You don't want an insubordinate or disruptive influence on others. You want to wow clients. You don't want to turn off customers. You want a positive work environment. Yes, Dead Wood is adding zero value. But is his behavior subtracting from your bottom line? As long as Dead Wood's impact is not negative, the answer is No, and it's okay to let it go. Don't let Dead Wood take your eyes off the ball. He may be a personal problem for you, but Dead Wood may not be a business problem for your organization. Sufficient for the company is its own success. Truth, Justice, and the American Way are Superman's business, and should not be among your top priorities. So coach yourself to do nothing. A physician will warn you that if you see a person stabbed in the chest, you shouldn't rush to pull the knife out.

Poor fit happens for four main reasons. Let me go through them briefly.

First, poor fit occurs when the recruitment and selection process is based on quality control that is feedback rather than feedforward. Feedback control is designed to correct hiring mistakes once they have been made. Feedforward control emphasizes the importance of avoiding mistakes before they happen. Traditionally, many more organizations favor feedback rather than feedforward control in screening, selecting, and managing their work force. The overall outcome would be the same if firing or laying-off an employee happened to be as easy to accomplish as hiring an employee. All things considered, is it easier to downsize or upsize? In today's working world, as you have already experienced and we will discuss at length in a few minutes, getting rid of Dead Wood is becoming more and more difficult.

Furthermore, in an age of padded resumes, exaggerated accomplishments, dishonest references, and falsified credentials, quality control that is feedforward as opposed to feedback may be more demanding and challenging, but all the more necessary. In the end, organizations that persist in managing backward rather than forward to control the size and quality of their work force will accumulate more Dead Wood. It would make more sense to avoid hiring the wrong people in the first place. That may seem self-evident, but so does the simple-minded axiom that fools hire fools, and that, too, happens every day.

Second, poor fit is the result of movement within the organization. For example, how many newly-minted CEOs, or managers with any other job title or authority-level, assuming leadership of a company or work group for the first time, begin their reign by undertaking a wave of reorganization or restructuring of people and positions? No one really knows. But the best guess is all of them. New bosses tend to "shuffle the deck." Productivity, efficiency, and morale usually do not get any better. But that is not the real reason for reorganizing. The first thing that a new boss needs to do to prove himself to his boss is to show that he can "hit the ground running." Reorganizing says to everyone, "There is a new sheriff in town, and a new sheriff means new rules." If you cannot make things better, then make things different. Some workers receive a promotion. Some are transferred to a brand-new job. Some have assignments and responsibilities added on to or subtracted from their current work role. Some keep doing the same job, but assigned to a different supervisor and given new reporting lines.

An organization is like a chessboard: "All the mistakes are there, just waiting to be made."

Third, poor fit also occurs naturally, not just because of new leadership. Socialized all their lives to be all that you can be, workers aspire ever upward. Dr. Laurence J. Peter famously observed in his best-selling classic of 25 years, "The Peter Principle," that Corporate America drives workers relentlessly upward until they eventually achieve a position that they simply cannot perform satisfactorily. And there they withdraw, day after day, foot-dragging and goofing-off. Similarly, C. Northcote Parkinson's celebrated "laws" state that when the time and money available to accomplish a task increase, so does overstaffing and make-work jobs.

Still, the net result is always the same. People land in the wrong job because of a poor fit between their talents, interests, and needs versus the demands and expectations of their new position.

Finally, time brings human changes. According to recent biological studies, human beings undergo continuous qualitative change. The human organism changes its entire physical make-up every seven years. This means that seven years from now, no atom or molecule in your body today will still be there, because new ones will have replaced all of them.

And our consciousness is in constant change as well. Workers lose interest in their job and become uncaring. Workers develop new emotional and spiritual voids that their current job description cannot fill. Workers develop new skills and talents and feel stifled and underemployed. Existentialism, the philosophical movement that stresses man's existence is a void, and people are totally free to change into whatever they want to be, suggests that in the long run, a poor fit between the kind of person you are becoming and the kind of job you do is as inevitable as mud on a pig.

What is a changing man to do in a clinging job? The Buddha would answer, "Become unhappy, unproductive, and useless Dead Wood."

Management is usually well trained in how to reward good performers and eliminate incompetent workers, those employees who "fit in the box." But they don't know how to deal with employees who are stuck in the middle, who are mediocre, second-rate performers because they just aren't suited for the job due to a mismatched personality or skill-set.

Survival Norm #6: Lose Your Illusions!
Of all the false ideas and misleading images that lead people astray and take them down one dead-end street after another, the greatest of these is free will. It gives us a great deal of emotional and spiritual satisfaction to believe that our actions are being consciously decided from one moment to the next and that human behavior is completely the result of free choices and decisions, rather than being compelled by impersonal cause-and-effect relationships over which we possess neither control nor influence. Given the same situation again, we believe that blessed with the distinctly human capacity to change our mind, we can simply say No! and choose to behave differently. No!

to society's roles and rules. No! to the demands and expectations of others. No! to everything. Human behavior is free and totally unfettered from moment to moment and we are in control. Bullfeathers! The argument over the existence of free will is over. Science has reached a verdict, and it's unanimous. Yes, free will does exist, but only as a fantasy or illusion, like Santa Claus or the Easter Bunny, and not as a real, empirical thing. "Science Times," in an article published in January 2007, quoted an authority on this subject as saying, "The conscious mind is like a monkey riding a tiger of subconscious decisions and actions, making up stories about being in control." And if we have so little control of the inner forces that drive and shape our own actions and behavior, how much control can we hope to acquire over the behavior of others? Using the tools and techniques in this and other perceptive self-help books to modify your own behavior to your advantage will never be easy, but I am confident that it is not impossible. After all, many people feel so inspired by Oprah that they manage to break their old eating habits and lose weight. Transforming other people to Fire Wood from Dead Wood will require a lot more hard work and hard attention than buying fat-free potato chips, but it can be done. Schopenhauer, the German philosopher said a person can do what he wants to do, but he cannot will what he wants to do. But I say that a monkey can sometimes motivate a tiger to change direction. If you will what I want you to do, then others will do what you want them to will.

Four:
Enough is too many:

Although all organizations can afford to employ a certain amount of Dead Wood, without undermining their long-term success and prosperity, the accumulation of Dead Wood cannot go on forever. That's because the mission of the organization has to be accomplished by everyone else, that is to say, by the Fire Wood. And that's why Dead Wood *loves* Fire Wood. Because if there is too much Dead Wood, then that will leave too little Fire Wood to pursue the organization's goals and achieve the organization's success. Translation: Bye-bye free ride.

In the average organization, what is the "elbow point" at which the organization's future progress or near-term survival is at risk? In other words, how much Dead Wood is too much Dead Wood?

Statistically, the best estimate that can be given concerning the distribution of any variable in a given population is described by the shape of a normal or bell curve of probabilities, in which the long, thin tails on both ends represent extremely rare outcomes. That means if you picture the job performance continuum discussed earlier, and superimpose a bell curve, then an organization's work force can be broken down into three basic groups of employees. At one end of the continuum is a small percentage of the work force made up of top performers, the company's all-stars and MVPs. At the opposite end of the continuum are an equally small percentage of workers consisting of the incompetents and the unemployables. Long-term, personnel decisions regarding these two groups of employees are obvious and practically make themselves. Retain, reward, and promote the former versus remediate, demote, and terminate the latter.

You will recall that Dead Wood is characterized by job performance that is neither satisfactory enough nor unsatisfactory enough to be identified with either extreme. It is in the bulge, in the middle of the curve, imbedded in the third and largest group of workers, among the borderline nincompoops and the near-great performers, that Dead Wood is found. As useless Dead Wood displaces more and more of the organization's productive Fire Wood, just as water displaces air when an open vessel is submerged, a visible, measurable decline in organizational success can easily be predicted.

Rain does not pour from an empty sky. When you see productivity or efficiency or customer service or any other deliverables continue to decline, despite Fire Wood's best efforts to reverse course, take cover! Your organization has been carrying too much Dead Wood and the end is near. Dead Wood has hijacked your organization.

If you know how to read the signs of the times, then you can find a trail of clues leading to a more exact, numerical ratio of Dead Wood to Fire Wood even in the pre-globalized, post-modern, 21st century, disinformation age.

One in ten HP workers is Dead Wood.

In 2005, both the "New York Times" and "Wall Street Journal" reported that over the following 18 months, Hewlett-Packard, the giant computer and printer maker, suffering from slow growth and inconsistent results, would lay off 14,500 employees, about 10% of its global work force. Identified by the company as "support" or "redundant" are the majority of those losing their jobs.

One of every three white-collar workers at Ford is Dead Wood.

According to the "Wall Street Journal" in 2005, Ford Motor Company, in the fourth year of a turnaround plan, has announced deep cuts in its North American work force over the next few years that will eliminate 10,500 or about 30% of all current white-collar positions. "We realize we have cost performance issues, and we are going to address them," said a Ford spokesman of the plan to trim the company's management by almost a third.

Down the road, if you see good things happening at HP or Ford despite massive downsizing, that's a neat unobtrusive indicator that in separating the sheep from the goats, in discriminating between Fire Wood and Dead Wood, the company has chosen pretty wisely.

Of course, if you have to work with Dead Wood day after day, one case study feels like too many. Unfortunately, Dead Wood doesn't always hew to the shape of a bell curve. Be afraid, be very afraid of a "fat tail." A fat tail would mean that there is actually much more Dead Wood in the company than one would guess given a normal work force. That's where the abnormal is so abnormal it begins to feel normal.

Five:
How to spot Dead Wood
in the cult of busyness:

It would be fashionable to say that spotting Dead Wood is a lot like the U.S. Supreme Court looking for pornography: Difficult to describe, but you will know it when you see it. That may be true, but it is not very enlightening or practical business advice you can take away and use to address the day in, day out personal and professional challenges of the Dead Wood phenomenon.

Frankly, Dead Wood boils down to seven different personas, or types of work roles, that can be easy to spot once you have studied their profiles and understand what to look for. It's not as difficult as finding a needle in a haystack. It's more like finding one dwarf among seven Snow Whites.

Let me lay out a short, vivid snapshot of the main features of each one. Each type of Dead Wood should be treated like a brand, made up of a cluster of defining brand-attributes. On the one hand, one particular personality profile may describe to a T your personal Dead Wood experience in the office down the hall or on the other side of your cubicle wall. On the other hand, to best describe your close encounter of the Dead Wood kind, a certain combination of attitudes and behaviors derived from two or more profiles may be needed. Either way, think of each profile as a lens that focuses one's attention on what to look for in front of you and what to expect behind your back. And remember that any classification of human personalities is like renovating an old house: The more work you finish, the more work remains to be done. As my seventh-grade teacher, Mrs. Tenpenny, put it, "Wisdom is not filling a bucket, but lighting a fire."

The Politician

"Gossip is power."

The Politician is a type of Dead Wood that spends most of his time and attention on the job busily hoarding and storing away information of all kinds. You don't ever have to tell The Politician what is going on, because he already knows more than you do. The Politician has rumored every rumor. The Politician has tattled every tale. The Politician has gossiped every shred of gossip. The Politician knows every company secret that is worth knowing. Sociologically speaking, The Politician helps clarify and reinforce the norms and values that keep people working well together by exposing those who cheat and deceive. It is by no means easy work, being everyone's favorite informer. "Did you know that one of your subordinates is cheating on his wife?" "Would you like me to tell you which one of your colleagues is hiding a drinking problem?" "Is *she* gay?" "One of the big shots is about to be fired and doesn't have a clue. Would you like to know if it's you?" The Politician can sense which kinds of "talking out of school" are most likely to win attention and gain acceptance. The Politician spreads inside information about the character and behavior of co-workers that cannot be published on an organizational chart or in an HR handbook, but "stuff" you need to know and can't learn anywhere else. "Is so-and-so dependable?" "Is he trustworthy?" "Does he take credit for other people's work?" The Politician is always tuned in, and can tell what gossipers are chitchatting about and what inquiring minds want to know. "Is the company for sale?" "Is the boss retiring this year?" "When are they giving us our annual bonus?" "Is the CEO in trouble with the board?" He is constantly shopping for and stockpiling scraps of insider information like a raccoon in a picnic basket, and darting from one employee to another like a crazed bumblebee. But The Politician is more than willing to leak his secrets to you for more and better secrets. The Politician controls the flow of gossip and holds a lot of power. He can be devious, and is known to have spread false rumors in order to manipulate others. The Politician knows everyone on a first-name basis, and networks constantly, but he shares his secrets "just between you and me." The Politician confides in everyone, and therefore no one. Off the record, his "job" is to be privy to what everyone else is doing, thinking, and saying behind the backs of their colleagues and co-workers, and The Politician is an infinite ocean of buzz. If it is none of your business, then it is The Politician's business. It used to be, and even in the age of online Weblogs still is, that if you want to know what it is really like to work for any company, then you need to have a friend on the inside. Someone who can share war stories and first-person glimpses into the day-to-day organization – a world that only an employee in the ranks ever gets to see. That is the source of The Politician's value and influence. The Politician's motto, "I will know the truth, and the truth will set me free from doing my job."

Survival Norm #7: Be Wary of Office Idols and Cubicle Gods!

For all of us, what we look for in our work, what we desire and need to feel happy and fulfilled are based on experiences from our past. If a person feels insecure and vulnerable because earlier he was hurt or wounded unjustly by criticism or attack, then he will look for a combination father figure and street fighter who knows the arena and understands how to outfox the lions to shield and protect his friends and allies. That's why so many people are so readily drawn to The Politician and admire him as a wise adviser, cunning advocate, and most valuable friend. The Politician is a magnet for people who are looking to fill in an old gap in their past working relationships. When people bind themselves to The Politician, in their own minds, it means they have outsourced a dirty, dangerous job and that frees them from taking responsibility for it themselves. The Politician sacrifices his job to office politics so that not everyone will have to, and for that sacrifice, The Politician is placed on a pedestal and idolized as an office god. The good news is that the higher the pedestal, the greater the fall. The bad news is that the closer you are to The Politician, the easier it is to see his flaws, but that pedestal can get pretty darn high. Once people form an attachment to a special person, and get involved, it becomes too costly to admit to making a lousy choice, and back away, so they see only the good and cannot see the bad and stick to their commitment. The problem is that people will come to believe that The Politician's way is The Way and that politics alone can pave the way to their future success. Up With Politics! Down With Work! The solution is to motivate people to break their bond

with a colleague perceived as smart, caring, and valuable
— difficult, not impossible. People often sever their ties with
close friends and even family members. There are many
more important things that people care about and are not
willing to sacrifice to their relationship, so they sacrifice
their relationship instead. People are not willing to sacrifice
their values, their dignity, their self-respect, or their pride,
so sacrificing their relationship is worth it to them. Yes, it
is a letdown, and there is grief. But the pain of staying in
the relationship becomes greater than the pain of severing
ties. To defeat a god, you must become god. To defeat The
Politician, you must convert his followers. The bond between
The Politician's disciples and their supreme being is based
on mutual exchange and reciprocity, pure and simple. Their
relationship will be strong and last only as long as it is cost-
effective. You must convince them that their relationship
with The Politician is more than they bargained for, and that
his way is not what they think it is. Preach that company
politics is real. And it's an important thing. But it's not
the only important thing and it's not the most important
thing. At worst, company politics leads to meaninglessness,
alienation, and self-estrangement. At best, company politics
leads to success without pride, prestige without honor,
reward without achievement, and title without respect.
Pride, Honor, Achievement, Respect: If you put a price
on their relationship with The Politician that is more than
people are willing to pay, then they will back out.

The Postman

"You can't spell T-E-A-M without M-E."

The Postman is a type of Dead Wood that never produces anything of real value, because he delegates all of his assignments and responsibilities to others who do his work for him. Good managers are supposed to spread the kudos and take the blame. The Postman takes all of the kudos and applause, but pushes down all of the blame. The Postman's "work" is to delegate his work to other people ... then take the credit for their sacrifices and achievements. He no longer has a legitimate job description, because little by little and piece by piece, The Postman has parceled out his workload to subordinates and co-workers. You don't have to be in a management position to be The Postman, but underlings make excellent enablers, for obvious reasons. They want to trust their boss, and they can't complain. The executive who always insists on bringing his subordinates along with him to every important meeting with his boss or his peers is not promoting workplace democracy. He is dumbing-down his job description to that of serving as a go-between or middleman. The Postman's make-believe "job" is to monitor and facilitate the real work of his subordinates, reasoning, "My staff should be by my side at all times and attend every working meeting with me. Since my subordinates are going to be doing the work for me, they may as well be in on the planning to hear my/their work assignments firsthand. (Read: If anything should go terribly wrong, my staff will be blamed, not me.)" The Postman is not above making unethical use of one of his more competent subordinates, by enhancing or elevating that employee above his teammates, and delegating the executive's workload mainly to him. Interpreted by his teammates as favoritism, and initially flattering, it is in fact gross exploitation, and soon looks and feels that way, too.

The Postman often finds a home in the top positions in business and industry. For many years, one senior executive was widely known and well respected in my company for energetically taking detailed notes at every meeting or group discussion, as if he was always deeply and thoroughly engaged in the agenda at hand. After he retired, hundreds of notebooks were found in his office … containing page after page of crossword puzzles, all neatly filled in.

When you see The Postman coming toward you, run as fast as you can in the other direction. Because The Postman is delivering a new job for you to do: His. And no job is impossible for The Postman who doesn't have to do it. As your leader, The Postman's motto is, "Follow me! I will be behind you every step of the way. We're all in this alone!"

Survival Norm #8: The Check is in the Mail

Work flows down. Praise floats up. In essence, that's The Postman's inner gyroscope. Every Abler requires an Enabler, and because you do great work and he can bask in the reflected glory of your successes, The Postman has chosen you. You didn't choose The Postman, but by catching The Great Delegator's passes and consistently running for a touchdown, you have inadvertently appointed yourself to be his favorite receiver. The spirit may be weak, but the flesh is willing and able. Any human will tend to repeat behavior if it is followed by positive reinforcement. The more accomplished you are, the more successful The Postman becomes, and the more positive reinforcement he gets. The result of all this is that it becomes more and more difficult for you to change the way The Postman treats you. You could try mixing a few fumbles with your successes. But to do less than the best you can do is not who you are. Besides, it can hardly be called an achievement when the operation is a success (because The Postman stops stuffing your inbox) but the patient dies (because your good name and reputation are spoiled). And you would only discover the hard way what social scientists have known for a long, long time, that intermittent rewards are even more reinforcing than constant rewards. The solution is to find the hidden check in The Postman's mail. To be the kind of person willing to do The Postman's job for him, and able to do it well, you must be the kind of person who enjoys the doing. Responsibility is what The Postman has given you. Authority is what you must take. You must make all decisions and your decisions must be final. You, the person in the field doing the work must be in charge, and not The Postman in his office. There is no other way. Responsibility without authority is indefensible, no question. Once you have both his authority and responsibility, it is only a matter of time before you have The Postman's title, paycheck, and corner office. To get the job you want, you must do the job you want, not the one you have. Don't resist The Postman. Just do it. Dress yourself for his position. And help The Postman unwittingly groom his successor – you!

The Therapist

"Work is pulling us apart. Love will keep us together."

The Therapist is a type of Dead Wood that never fails to celebrate a major holiday. The Therapist never forgets a colleague's birthday. The Therapist never misses an opportunity to bring cake and punch and party in the office. You had forgotten that your wedding anniversary is the day after tomorrow, until The Therapist reminded you. In November, The Therapist decorates the office with plastic turkeys and in December, candy canes. To celebrate Halloween, The Therapist insists that everyone dress for work as a "Star Wars" character. When your son was injured in a mineshaft explosion, The Therapist donated blood and cried with you. When your wife almost caught you cheating with another woman, The Therapist was your alibi. The Therapist covered for you when you spent last Friday at a Yankees' game "working from home." When you found a lump in your breast, The Therapist took you to the hospital and waited hours for you. Every morning, The Therapist spends a couple of hours socializing at the coffee machine and strolling leisurely from office to office backslapping, handholding, and bonding. The Therapist's job is to keep his colleagues company in the office. The Therapist spends a couple of hours more each day online, exchanging e-mail messages about Oprah with fellow workers, transmitting electronic greeting cards, and trading cookie recipes. When the going gets tough, The Therapist makes everyone waffles. Good waffles, too! With fruit toppings and whipped cream!

The Therapist is Everyman's mother, father, brother, sister, and best friend. Work-time is fun-time. And The

Therapist's "job," in his own individual way, is to establish, maintain, and protect employee morale. The Therapist's creed: "An organization is not about work. Work is just an excuse to bring people together. It is all about Family."

Survival Norm #9: Great Teams Can't Win Without Great Workers and Great People

Managers have many different, demanding jobs to do. However, there is no other managerial responsibility that is more important, more valuable, and more necessary than building a winning team. And to accomplish that, you can't just recruit good workers. You need good people, too. You need The Therapist. A good worker draws a straight line between where he is and where he wants to be and then grinds to dust anything and anyone that stands in his way. The greatest worker is a machine, and machines make excellent tools for getting things done, but they make for lousy relationships. Enlightened managers can do much to develop great workers in the workplace. That's the whole purpose behind mandating regular performance appraisals. That's not necessarily a bad thing. Great workers fuel productivity. The Therapist's unselfish caring and concern for the happiness and well-being of his teammates may not strike you at first as a legitimate job description. But The Therapist and his "work" are an unproductive inconvenience that quickly become a productive necessity. Altruism, such as The Therapist has, develops almost from the moment of birth. The problem of The Therapist as well as the solution to The Therapist are one and the same! Given the intimate work environment, and the long, stressful hours that people put in at work today, most everyone needs to find a way to release the intense pressure. Emotionalizing, romanticizing, and, finally, eroticizing work relationships provides both relief and pure team-building. Don't try to overrule The Therapist. Because teamwork starts with the need to relate and belong to each other. That means individual satisfaction must take precedence over productivity, and happiness over morale. Interaction and communication must be personal as well as professional. Relationships must be deep, extensive, and last beyond the specific task or goal at hand. The Therapist's work environment is an infinite ocean of inner meaning, feeling, and emotion. No question, it will consume a great deal of time and involve a lot of sharing of feelings and personal interests and talking about the work vs. doing the work. But that is the glue from which the strongest, most productive teams are made. The Therapist's job is to be the source and consciousness of the we-feeling, transforming great workers into a great team, and a great team into family.

The Beaver
"Great smoke. Little fire."

The Beaver is a type of Dead Wood that is always very busy, so busy in fact that The Beaver has no time to get anything done. The Beaver is, as strange as this may sound, too busy doing his job to do his job. That's because The Beaver insists on doing everything, and doing everything by himself. He commits to every project. He sits on every committee. He attends every meeting. He volunteers for projects no one else wants. No job is too big, no deadline too short, for The Beaver to take on. The Beaver is always running late from his last meeting, and has to leave early to be on time for his next one. Results? "I'm working on it," means, "I haven't started yet." "I'll have it finished by tomorrow," means, "Two weeks, maybe." "I'm thinking about it," means, "I haven't thought about it." "I'll get back to you," means, "Never." The Beaver delegates nothing. He is incapable of prioritizing. The Beaver's office is littered with dusty piles of random paperwork, half-finished reports, unread memos, and unsigned requisitions. The Beaver's Ph.D. really means Piled High and Deep. Do you remember that purchase request you sent to The Beaver's office for his signature last month? I hope you retained a copy. The Beaver's e-mail account has exceeded its storage limit and now is automatically trashing the unopened message you transmitted to him weeks ago. Do not bother telephoning The Beaver because he will not be available to take your call, and his voicemail box is full and will not accept new messages. Do not bother asking for a meeting either, because his calendar already contains more "conflicts" than the Middle East. I would let you speak with The Beaver's secretary, but she is on sick leave.

His co-workers admire the Beaver because he is so hard working and energetic. Yes, it is true that The Beaver is busy. However, he is not productive. Disorganized and unfocused, The Beaver cannot seem to follow through to successful completion and execute. The Beaver manages to get by creating a thick fog of extreme busyness to fill the void of real accomplishment, fooling most everyone. The Beaver's motto, "There is more job security in ten half-finished tasks than in five completed ones."

Survival Norm #10: A Fix for the Work Addict

The Beaver is not simply a person who is so dedicated to doing a good job that he is obsessively busy. The Beaver is hooked on work, and just like a drug addict, is unable to turn work off. The Beaver puts work before family and personal life. He devotes so much time to work and puts in such long hours that he cannot see his family or meet and socialize with significant others. If you manage to find The Beaver in a social setting, his conversation and chitchat will be dominated by work. The Beaver works from home after every workday ends. And weekends, vacations, and holidays are used for getting caught up, getting ahead, or getting prepared for work. He sleeps with his BlackBerry and checks it throughout the night. Removed from work and unable to feed his habit, it is common for The Beaver to experience physical and psychological withdrawal symptoms such as anger, depression, headaches, as well as sleep and eating disorders. Neglected relationships with family and friends cannot be sustained, so they suffer and are sacrificed to work. The problem is that The Beaver is wholeheartedly convinced that only he can do the work that needs doing. That's why he feels so comfortable controlling every big job and every little task, and feels so much discomfort delegating. Cold turkey is not the answer. The solution is to show The Beaver how to control with delegating rather than delegating with the risk of losing control. The first step is to make The Beaver establish his No. 1 goals and top priorities. Make sure that The Beaver picks a doable number of important goals. The second step is to make The Beaver define the actions that need to be taken and tasks that need to be completed to achieve each goal. Make sure that The Beaver is both *careful to include only those tasks that support his goals and specific about actions that need to be taken on a daily basis. The third step is to make The Beaver identify all of the leftover work that remains to be done but that doesn't support and facilitate his highest priorities. The last step is to assign those tasks that don't help a lower priority and cast them away. They are getting in the way, cluttering The Beaver's workday, and should be delegated. By making The Beaver sort out his top priorities, and declutter the rest by delegating, The Work Addict can still get his work-fix and own those tasks that support his goals. But he can also free up time and attention to follow through and finally finish something, just by giving up the stuff that was never really that important to him in the first place.*

The Empire Builder
"The spirit is willing, but the flesh is underfunded."

The Empire Builder is a type of Dead Wood that cannot accomplish much of anything, but don't blame him, because it is not his fault. Complaining nonstop that he is deprived of the necessary resources, The Empire Builder requires more staff, more money, more equipment, and more space – in short, more of everything before he can do his job. The Postman pushes his job away from himself and on the backs of others. The Empire Builder draws everything into himself. That's why he needs more and more and more. But no matter how many additional resources are allocated to him, enough is never enough for the needy Empire Builder. If he begins work on an assignment, then it is only a matter of time before The

Empire Builder holds it hostage, demanding that he does not have the resources required to complete the project. Gimme! Gimme! Gimme! I need! I need! I need! Should The Empire Builder finish the job successfully, then hallelujah, Praise the Lord, it was only by walking on water, and he cannot be expected to do it again. Gimme! The Empire Builder is notorious for purposely falling short of success just to "prove" that he was right in the first place. And when co-workers complain that The Empire Builder is not doing his job, and everyone else has to work harder to make up the difference, that also proves he was right all along.

The Empire Builder is forever understaffed, underequipped, underfunded, overworked, and over budget. Only after hiring additional staff, receiving a substantial budget increase, relocating to a larger office, and purchasing new equipment, nags The Empire Builder, will he be able to get his job done. "I am doing as much as I can with what I have been given to work with. You cannot ask me to do the impossible. I want to be able to do more, but until I have more resources, you will just have to do it yourself, or find another way of meeting your needs."

The Empire Builder cannot get enough of what he doesn't really want. The Empire Builder's motto, "Help me help you help me."

Survival Norm #11: A**hole is NOT a Figure of Speech!
People who hoard all sorts of valued things, like ideas,
money, access, praise, and relationships, are among
the most destructive and frustrating members of any

organization. They kill teamwork and team spirit and every other type of social groupness. They sow mistrust and suspicion. They shut down open communication and the free exchange of information. They inflame individualism and undermine community. They turn a company into a war of all, against all. Freud described this type of personality as "anal" and this behavior as "anal retentive." Freud explained that in early childhood, The Empire Builder had a deep-seated need to feel safe by establishing a sense of control over the important people and things around him. But The Empire Builder was never able to establish that sense of control and overcome his feelings of powerlessness and insecurity. Withholding all sorts of important things in adulthood is The Empire Builder's way of fulfilling his earlier unfulfilled desire for power and control over his environment. Begging or trying to force him to share control or access are a hopeless waste of time. You will not be able to use your feelings of insecurity to satisfy his need to feel safe. The solution is not to overcome The Empire Builder's sense of powerlessness, but to encourage and reinforce it! During his rare, unguarded moments of trust, you must show The Empire Builder that people are working around him, that people are turning to others to acquire the resources they need, that the job is getting done without him, that people don't need him, that he no longer influences and controls the people around him, and that he is less secure and more powerless than ever. You must show The Empire Builder that by hoarding access to valued resources, he is actually losing control of his work role, work relationships, and work environment. You must show The Empire Builder that opening up is his best hope of controlling things. You must show him that controlling people and their behavior is easier and more effective when they are needy and you have needful things to give. If you want The Empire Builder to loosen up, then just show him how well drug dealers and drug addicts work together. Now that's his idea of reciprocity!

The Figurehead

"100 percent of work is showing up."

The Figurehead is a type of Dead Wood that, having no real power or authority, adds much the same value to any work activity as an article of furniture, a potted plant, or a statue. The Figurehead is an empty suit that occupies space and has weight, but do not expect much more from him than visibility. An ambassador, he earns his paycheck just by showing up and shaking hands. Like a Black Hole in outer space, he exists and exerts a spooky attraction on everything around him, but no one can really explain how or why. Home for The Figurehead is on Mt. Olympus, in the clouds above the day-to-day nuts-and-bolts of the company's operation. Figuratively, that is, meaning that the routine processes and functions required to transform raw inputs into marketable outputs, and the toilers who roll up their sleeves and sweat over them, the organization's bread and butter, are not important enough to deserve the interest and attention of The Figurehead. But also literally, because The Figurehead's office is often located on one of the uppermost floors of a tall building, in the heavens, segregated far, far above the company's laborers and their instrumentation. The workers and their work are beneath him in every way. If employed by a hospital, then The Figurehead could not care any less about physicians and patients. If the organization is a university, then a classroom or laboratory filled with teachers and students is the last place one should expect to find The Figurehead. And in a factory, the assembly line never creates a blip on The Figurehead's radar. Know-how, possessing the technical skill and hands-on experience to understand the business and contribute to the bottom line, is for "the little people." Even when he is speaking to you about your job, he leaves you with the impression that he is just there to punch your ticket and have his ticket punched by you. The Figurehead is busy with "special projects" and made-up jobs that have true, lasting value only to the extent to which they keep The Figurehead too occupied to meddle in something he knows nothing about, namely, the work. American workers like to believe that their boss is a lazy, uncaring idiot who could not do their job if his life depended on it. But they also want to believe just as strongly that their boss's boss is hard-working, dedicated, intelligent, and true-blue. Not The Figurehead. Take a look at why he is on your payroll and how he spends his time: Building heart-to-heart relationships with local politicians; Sponsoring charitable organizations to save mankind; Leaving no child behind; Supporting the arts. Sound worthwhile, don't they? Until you look behind the hype, and The Figurehead's role is deciding menus, dress codes, and seating charts for banquets and cocktail parties. Fitting work for someone who is, after all, The Bench-Warmer of the Working World. And the meetings. Oh, the meetings. Too big. Too long. Start with banal pep talks. End with banal pep talks. Hijack the topic at hand. Try to prove everyone else wrong. Impress the superiors who are present. Blather on and on for his own enjoyment. And the agenda? Well, have you heard The Figurehead's two-hour PowerPoint presentation of his cost-benefit analysis of mechanical pencils versus manual pencils? Dead-end, make-work assignments, call it "Administrivia," are The Figurehead's calling. If management is a joke, he is the punch line. His tools-of-the-trade are the tuxedo, the brunch, the vodka martini, and his titanium golf clubs. Do I have to draw you a picture? Okay, imagine the Scarecrow on his way to Oz wearing a business suit and carrying a briefcase.

The Figurehead's motto, "No job too small, no salary too big."

Survival Norm #12: Is the Suit Half-filled or Half-empty?

The Figurehead may not have brains, integrity, or accomplishments, but he's got personality. Personality so big and magnetic that it has played the most significant role in his success, and The Figurehead has been getting ahead only because of it. How big is it? All too often, The Figurehead manages to backslap and ha-ha his way to the top, even into the corner office. People want to believe that it is a just world, and that these empty suits eventually get the boot. And while this deeply-held belief does give people a great deal of emotional and spiritual satisfaction, it's pure fantasy-building. The truth is that the heart is stronger than the head, and The Figurehead's charisma and yahoo personality has won legions of friends and loyal supporters. He may be achieving little, but who would you rather follow, Mr. Spock or Dr. McCoy? The fact is that great intelligence cannot succeed without some charisma. But enough charisma can be a great success without intelligence. It's not how good you are, but how good you look. That's the bad news. The good news is that every company needs The Figurehead. Because only he can make certain important jobs a whole lot easier. A wow personality even with a d'oh mind is ideal in critical situations that require firing up people and inspiring them. When people need to be energized and moved, scientific reason and geometric logic are much less effective than naked passion and raw emotion. Cheerleaders carry pom-poms, not calculators. Every day, companies must convince their employees and customers that change is good even when it hurts. How do you convince people to swallow good medicine that tastes bad? You can reason with them. But people have a strong, natural resistance to change. Overcoming that resistance requires personal magnetism and the ability to flatter, charm, coax, humor, seduce, enlist, and woo. It can't be done by reasoning alone. It takes pure personality. The Figurehead is an empty suit, but you must learn to see him as being half-filled rather than half-empty. Gameshow hosts don't need the answers to play the game, they need winning personalities to keep the game in play.

The Bottleneck
"Success is not an option."

The Bottleneck is a type of Dead Wood that does not oppose new ideas, but he does not support them. He does not resist change, but he does not implement it. He makes decisions, but he does not execute them. He does not get things done, but he gets them documented. That's because The Bottleneck is unconcerned with who takes the credit. He has learned that the higher one moves up the organization, the less control one has over anything, and the harder it is to get things done. What really matters is where you place the blame, and you have everyone but yourself to blame. The Bottleneck believes that success means not failing. You are a success as long as you cannot be blamed for failure when something misfires. Work is a blame-game. The Bottleneck blames because he lacks the skills to problem-solve. Problem-solving is about the future, and actions. Blame is about the past, and about labels. Hard decisions that could solve problems must be avoided. Success and accomplishment in the usual sense are an unjustifiable risk. Doing nothing eliminates any possibility of being blamed and, therefore, is always preferable to doing something and assuming the probability of failure, no matter how small. The Bottleneck's "job" is "covering yourself" because he has no results and cannot afford to be faulted for anything. So he wastes his time documenting every conversation, meeting, or work-related activity of any kind. He is conditioned to write memos and follow-up memos addressed to his own files to protect himself. He keeps written notes of every encounter no matter how casual with an incessant whiner or a known blabbermouth, scapegoater, saboteur, apple-polisher, or finger-pointer. He saves every old e-mail and voice-mail message as if they were splinters of the Cross. He takes "witnesses" with him to important discussions and decision-making meetings. The Bottleneck is a sign of the times. If you're unhappy, your spouse is to blame. If you're a loser, your parents are to blame. The Bible says even Paradise was filled with blame. After Eve ate the forbidden fruit, she blamed the serpent. Adam blamed Eve, and blamed God for giving him Eve. God blamed, well, you know the rest.

The old ideals of good management – plan, organize, lead, supervise, and control – have given way to a new philosophy that is entirely clerical. No job is too small that it does not get an elaborate paper trail. Call it "Bureaucrap." When forced to execute a high-impact decision or follow through on a new project, The Bottleneck will send out a memo detailing his forthcoming actions and require all other members of the team to sign-off on it. Because in The Bottleneck's world of work, there is a "law" that says you can only be blamed alone.

The Bottleneck's motto: "The absence of success is no reason for failure."

Tomayto. Tomahto.

Survival Norm #13: Set False Deadlines

The problem is that The Bottleneck is permitted to have the option to do work rather than fulfill the imperative to do work. Then The Bottleneck exercises that option by doing no work, which he finds can be better and more advantageous than doing it. The Bottleneck will accept responsibility for getting a job done, because he knows that no matter how long he takes to finish and no matter how late he is, there will be no unpleasant consequences. Using his logic, better never than late if never is still on time. That gives The Bottleneck license to downshift and work in slow motion by imposing unnecessary, self-serving steps that blame-proof his actions and decisions and trivialize the work flow. The solution is to set deadlines – urgent, early, and false. Urgent, fire-alarm, do-or-die deadlines must be perceived to reflect high priorities and to be real. That means The Bottleneck must be afraid, be very afraid that busting the deadline on a top priority will hurt him badly. Early deadlines with no cushions built into them will force The Bottleneck to start the job by identifying what self-defense steps cannot be included in the work flow, rather than throwing in everything that could. Early deadlines do risk undermining the work product. But the higher the priority he believes his work to be, and the greater his fear of failure, the more justifiable the risk that the job won't turn out right. False deadlines fire up The Bottleneck to do real work for a change, and move at high speed. Besides, it's not a lie until the other person knows it's not true.

Six:
The Formal and Informal Organizations: Why Dead Wood is so difficult to get rid of:

In every organization, there are two houses.

In every position, there are two roles.

In every employee, there are two people.

In principle, regardless of mission or goals, size or complexity, age or history, all bureaucracies or work organizations are actually made-up of two institutions, separate and distinct, known to sociologists like myself as the Formal Organization and Informal Organization. Every large organization, whether it is a hospital, school, or factory, consists of two houses, the Formal Organization and Informal Organization, put together both in the processes that get things done and in the structure of the organization that becomes the structure of our own consciousness.

The Formal Organization and Informal Organization are very different from each other and each is composed of its own special rules and regulations, hierarchy of authority, division of labor, rights and privileges, and responsibilities and mutual expectations. Every position has its carefully defined and proper place in each house. As a result, every position actually consists of two different jobs or two different work roles. Every employee must take his designated seat on both sides of the organization. In fact, every employee is actually two different people with two different faces. He is one person as a member of the Formal Organization and an altogether different person as a member of the Informal Organization.

Let's keep it simple. Consider the Formal and Informal Organizations to be two opposite sides of the same coin, where both pictures are required to fully and completely describe and explain how the organization works. And in every employee, he has two pictures of himself, of the kind of person he is and is becoming. So, in general, to explain why workers behave as they do, both pictures, both identities have to be taken into consideration.

For our purposes, the most important differences between the Formal and Informal Organizations center on standards and criteria that determine successful and unsuccessful job performance.

Looking at every company's traditional organizational chart, containing lots of job titles in little boxes and compartments connected by solid and dotted reporting lines and arranged horizontally and vertically in relationship to authority, you are seeing the Formal Organization. Every employee in every box in the Formal Organization is graded against the same set of highly exalted and officially established norms and expectations. Written down, codified, explicitly acknowledged, and persistently reinforced throughout the organization in a thousand conspicuous ways, these are the supreme beings of the post-modern working world. Leadership. Vision. Productivity. Innovation. Problem Solving. Critical Thinking. Efficiency. Effectiveness. Enthusiasm. Teamwork. Team Building. Goal Setting. Goal Attainment. Dedication. Loyalty. Achievement.

Accomplishment. Courage. Almost from the moment of birth, we are socialized to serve these "gods." Take a closer look at the "progress reports" used to grade elementary-school students. There they are. Look in the faces of the Founding Fathers that stare down on your children from schoolroom walls, and in the portraits of company founders studying you from boardroom walls. There they are. And on these sacred ideals used to judge people and their behavior in the Formal Organization, Dead Wood has sinned and fallen short of heavenly glory, not to mention Wall Street and Madison Avenue.

Survival Norm #14: Control Your Ego!

Granted, the more success you have, the more your ego grows, and the very successful tend to have very big egos. Success may feed a hungry ego. However, that does not mean it takes a big, strong ego to become a great, big success. Your ego may swell with each victory, but if you truly believe that it is your ego that won it for you, instead of the kind of person you are and the kind of actions you take, then your ego will cost you dearly. Because once your ego grows too big and takes control, you will become convinced that you can win no matter who you are and how you play the game. And once you forget how you got where you are, you will be beaten. If you should win a few victories, once your ego is out of control, then you will even more easily be able to rationalize the worst decisions and bad behavior, leading to an even bigger defeat. As you succeed in overcoming Dead Wood or becoming immune to its consequences, the problem is how to keep your ego in check and remember what got you there. The solution is, first, to look carefully at every action and decision to make certain that you are not doing it for the wrong reason, namely, for pride. If your decision is ego-based, where your pride is, rather than reality-based, where the problem is, then your decision made for the wrong reason will always be the wrong decision. Second, as Alfred is to Bruce Wayne, Batman is to Robin. Find a mentor! A mentor is someone you like, trust, and respect who will tell you when you're heading off a cliff or down a dead-end street. Because when your ego is fed too much and grows too big, and your conscience is bound and gagged, and when you reach for your inner compass, it's not there, then you need to have your judgment of right and wrong audited by a wiser adviser. Success makes an ego, but failure takes an ego. When your ego becomes a bully, you must stand up to it!

The Informal Organization is another matter, and another world. Standards and expectations are very different there, even hostile to the Formal Organization.

The Formal Organization is task-oriented. The Informal Organization is people-oriented. In the Formal Organization, communication is expected to be written down and documented. In the Informal Organization, communication is expected to be casual, face-to-face, and by "the grapevine." Relationships between workers in the Formal Organization are expected to be impersonal, fleeting, and confined to tasks and professional goals. People are treated as means to an end. Relationships in the Informal Organization are expected to be deep, personal, and extensive, lasting and fulfilling, both emotionally and spiritually. People are treated as ends in themselves. A job well done is paramount in the Formal Organization. Happiness is paramount in the

Informal Organization. Work activities in the Formal Organization are clearly defined, highly specialized, and dictated by a rigid division of labor. Activities in the Informal Organization are much the same for all workers. In the Formal Organization, membership is based on technical competence to carry out assigned tasks. In the Informal Organization, membership is based on love and personal affection. The Formal Organization has a strict hierarchy of authority. In the Informal Organization, it is nonexistent. Everyone is equal.

The globalized, post-modern workplace is an assembly of strangers brought together from across oceans and cultures. But the organization's mission and plans can be accomplished by the Formal Organization only if within the Informal Organization workers demonstrate and exchange loyalty, mutual respect, altruism, faith, commitment, kindness, caring, and love. These are the goals of the Informal Organization. The Informal Organization is engendered by the wildly varying personalities of workers and their unique quirks, charisma, and character, and by their deep desire to relate and belong.

Your favorite baseball team, how you dress, and where your children go to school do not matter in the Formal Organization. But the kind of person you are is all that counts in the Informal Organization. And in an unnecessary and painful elaboration of the obvious, a great many scientific studies conducted over many years have consistently concluded that the Informal Organization is just as influential as the Formal Organization in determining organizational success and failure.

The bottom line: "I am more than the work I do. I am me."

Survival Norm #15: Believing is Seeing!

Reality is not in the mind. But thoughts are the stuff things are made of. Thinking is thinging. Because seeing other people and their behavior as they really are is much more than just a matter of opening our eyes and paying attention. The characteristics of the perceiving person actually govern and dictate what is perceived. First, our own personality and character determine the qualities we see in others, as well as our judgment of that appearance. We see traits and characteristics in others that we desire to possess in ourselves, but don't. Smart. Pretty. Successful. And the more profound and deeply felt those desires are, the more we look for and find those traits in others. We see desirable traits and characteristics in others that they possess in greater abundance than we do. Smarter. Prettier. More successful. We see what we want to be to complete ourselves and be all that we aspire to be. Second, the more self-accepting we are, the more favorable rather than unfavorable aspects of other people we tend to see, and the more favorable our judgment of them will be. Our self-feelings must be positive before our fellow-feelings will be. Accuracy in perceiving people is a skill like any other, to learn and develop. And knowing oneself makes it a lot easier to see others accurately. Dead Wood has many faces. First, you must untangle those unfulfilled desires and judgments you have about yourself from what you see. Whatever unfavorable traits and characteristics are left over must be real. Then you will know what needs doing and can focus on finding the right solutions to the right problems.

*This begins inside you, with the kind of person you are.
When you can look at Dead Wood and see beyond your
own reflection, you will have learned. Learned to see others
as they are, beyond what you are, and are not.*

Seven:
On the road to Damascus,
Dead Wood takes a short cut:

Ideally, individual, personal success ought to mirror organizational success. In other words, to be considered a success in the working world, a worker should have to be successful as a member of the Formal Organization, but also successful as a member of the Informal Organization. Successful job performance ought to mean that worker possesses both good social and people skills as well as good professional and technical skills. Role-playing and rule-following in the organization are both formal and informal as are the aspirations and achievements each worker is expected to pursue. Just as the organization is built on twin pillars, a successful worker should be a twin success. It is not enough to do the job right, you must be the right kind of person, too. In the perfect meritocracy, to paraphrase an old adage, it is what you know *and* what you are that count.

Ideally: Yes.

In the real-life working world: Not so fast. Actually, it is not only normal, "standard operating procedure," but also desirable to consider that worker a big success even though he has utterly failed as a member of the Formal Organization or the Informal Organization.

Think this sounds risky or impractical?

In general, the Formal Organization and the Information Organization each require every worker to satisfy different standards and expectations and to conform to different rules and norms of behavior.

For simplicity, let's assume that one's ability to fulfill the demands of the Formal Organization, call it "job performance," may be evaluated as either Satisfactory or Unsatisfactory, and the same is true for one's job performance in relationship to the demands of the Informal Organization. Furthermore, say that satisfactory job performance in the Formal Organization means, essentially, "Your work is good." And that unsatisfactory job performance in the Formal Organization means, "Your work sucks." Similarly, satisfactory job performance in the Informal Organization means, "Everyone likes you." While unsatisfactory job performance in the Informal Organization means, "No one likes you."

(For the moment, ignore what you have seen and we studied earlier about job performance being a continuum as opposed to a dichotomy, and just play along.)

Our thought-experiment yields four unique types of co-workers and work styles. For economy's sake, let's just call them Bob and Carol and Ted and Alice, based on the nature of one's job performance as a member of the Formal Organization and Informal Organization. They are:

> "Bob, your work is good, and everyone likes you."
>
> "Carol, your work sucks, but everyone likes you."
>
> "Ted, your work is good, but no one likes you."
>
> "Alice, your work sucks, and no one likes you."

Now suppose you are working in the HR and legal departments, what do you do next? The first two personnel decisions are easy to make. Reward, promote, raise, advance, elevate, upgrade, move up, and otherwise crown Bob. Bob is both competent and popular, one of the company's shooting stars, superheroes, and success stories. Then fire, decruit, oust, discharge, dismiss, delayer, cashier, drum out, give notice, lower the boom, terminate, decouple, can, sack, bounce, boot, ax, and pinkslip Alice. Alice is incompetent and unpopular, filling a much-needed void in the company.

In the perfect working world, Carol and Ted would also get the boot. Everyone is fond of Carol, but she has failed to fulfill her work role in the Formal Organization. While Ted was never accepted by the Informal Organization, but is a capable worker.

However, in today's real-life working world, Carol and Ted are often considered top-notch, first-rate performers, celebrated and rewarded among the organization's most talented assets, like Bob. That's the problem. Carol and Ted are hiding Dead Wood.

(By the way, if you would like a pretty accurate picture of how many Bobs, Carols, Teds, and Alices make up the work force of the typical organization, then just imagine the shape of a normal or bell curve like the one used earlier. There are fewer Bobs at one end of the curve, and fewer Alices at the other end. But between the stems, in the wave, found in the middle of the curve, there are a larger number of Carols and Teds. Holy Mackerel! Dead Wood. Take note that the curve will be more or less flat or steep depending on the specific organization. In short, beware of fat tails!)

Survival Norm #16: Beware of the Nonskill Skill and the Incompetency Competency

Overachievers will feign competencies they don't possess in order to qualify for more difficult, more challenging assignments that will add more value, burnish their image and reputation, and raise their profile to the next level. There are two kinds of lies. That's the good kind … where one's grasp exceeds one's reach. The bad kind occurs when underachievers feign incompetency in order to escape responsibility for value-added tasks and projects because they simply don't want to do them. They just don't feel like it. They can't be bothered. So they practice false incompetency. Dead Wood is a grandmaster of the skill of the nonskill. It's not that Dead Wood is incapable or incompetent. Dead Wood really is competent and really does understand how to do the job. But he claims not to understand and pretends to be so helpless that the job is reassigned and someone else gets stuck doing the work. Overachievers genuinely fear looking stupid. Underachievers are more than willing to prove it. The Hell of the Underachievers is where doing a good job on something you didn't want to do in the first place means getting trapped into doing it again and again. Planned incompetence looks like a crisis to those working around Dead Wood, but for him, it's a way out of one. The solution is to recognize and defend against feigned incapacity. No matter how simple and easy the job may be, you must learn to recognize Dead Wood's code for feigned dimwittedness.

He says:

"I haven't done this job for years. Help me remember how it should be done."

"This is so different from anything I've ever done. Teach me how to get started."

"This is way over my head. I'm so confused. I could learn so much from helping you."

"Who did this job last year?"

"I'll do my darnedest. I just hope I don't make too many mistakes."

"I assume there's no deadline."

"Show me how you would do this job if you were me."

"The last time I did this job the person who assigned me was fired."

"Would you mind writing down how it should be done?"

Once you recognize pseudo-incompetency, defending against it is easier. No matter what he says, you must not reassign the job from Dead Wood to anyone else!

You say:

"It's your job, period. Do your best."

People expect and even commend overachievers for wildly exaggerating their competencies to get ahead. But that coin has two sides, and incompetent competency is one of the most powerful performances in Dead Wood's repertoire. You must see through his theatricality, and not be deceived by pure dramatics. For Dead Wood, all the work's a stage, and all the men and women merely suckers.

Now, back to Carol and Ted.

Call it "the leveling process." In organizations or work settings where skill, expertise, experience, and record of accomplishment are standardized and do not vary meaningfully from worker to worker, where most everyone is doing a good job, the Informal Organization becomes much more important in separating the sheep from the goats, and the merely satisfactory from the meritorious. That means the kind of person you are, as implied by things like one's wardrobe, etiquette, neighborhood, and spouse, and the close friendships and alliances you have established, tend to carry a great deal of influence over how high up in the organization you can ascend. "Dressing for success" and "networking" and "coattailing" and "sleeping with the director" and "marrying the boss's daughter" – Social climbing does help advance modern careers, particularly in situations where success and achievement in the Formal Organization have become inadequate and ineffective in discriminating between the likes of Bob and Ted. As a rule of thumb, the more equality in the Formal Organization, the more inequality in the Informal Organization is emphasized to measure success and allocate future rewards.

Carol is regarded as a highly valuable employee, because, in some situations, the Informal Organization is treated with greater importance than it ought to be, and the Formal Organization as not important enough. Carol has become so popular and beloved that her incompetence as a member of the Formal Organization no longer matters. How could that happen? Carol sizes-up the situation correctly and then makes a perfectly rational choice. It goes like this. Carol finds that success in the Informal Organization is a necessary steppingstone for job security and career advancement. Carol also realizes that her performance as a member of the Formal Organization is lousy and will never rise to the level that merits the job rewards and upward mobility she desires. Therefore, Carol decides to invest most of her time, effort, and attention where it will do her the most good.

Carol learns to play "office politics" better than Bob. Carol wins more friends and allies than Bob. Carol is more outgoing and gregarious than Bob. Carol works harder at being needed and popular. Bob is a nice guy. Carol is super. Bob remembers birthdays. Carol brings the cake. Strategic Plan. Call Bob. United Way. Call Carol. Board Member. Call Bob. Dead Mother. Call Carol. Bob knows how to treat people "right." Carol knows how to treat "the right people." Bob's work has earned him the respect and recognition of higher-ups. Carol lives in the same neighborhood, joins the same country club, and makes sure their kids go to the same school. She has to. The Informal Organization is the one and only career path open to Carol to better herself.

It works. Everyone loves Carol! No one can even imagine the company without her. Go-To Guy: Bob. Sacred Cow: Carol. She receives the same salary increases as Bob. She is promoted with Bob. She enjoys the same job security as Bob. And in that situation, it is only a matter of time before Bob is working for Carol.

There is more than one right way of doing everything. Many more people assume that one's technical skills and accomplishments are the only path, the best path, the most desirable path, or the modal path to "the good things in life," wealth, prestige, power, pleasure, and personal fulfillment. When Carol eventually moves up into one of the top offices in the organization, these same people will be wondering how somehow so unqualified could have leapfrogged over the likes of Bob. Dead Wood often assumes the same kind of leadership role in the Informal Organization played by Fire Wood in the Formal Organization, and for the same reasons, hard work, determination, and proficiency. Organizations where excellence as a member of the Informal Organization obscures one's failings in the Formal Organization will be crammed with Carols.

In today's other-directed organizational culture, the road to career success increasingly detours through the Informal Organization, and more careers blossom because of knowing the right people rather than because of knowing the right stuff. Conversely, more careers have dead-ended because of who you don't know than because of what you don't know.

Which boss or co-worker would you rather have? Carol or Ted? A likeable idiot or a brilliant jerk?

Many other organizations emphasize the importance of the Formal Organization at the expense of or even to the exclusion of the Informal Organization. In these situations, one's success in the Formal Organization can easily add so much value that one's weaknesses and deficiencies as a member of the Informal Organization become inconsequential. It is here that Teds flourish. His personality sucks, but Ted is a money-maker and cash cow. He may have the relationship-building skills of a fern, but Ted is a winner. Christmas is Christmas. Business is business. It's called The Human *Race*. Nice guys finish last. Ted is not a people-person, so, they say, he can all the more focus like a laser beam on formal tasks and goals, and that makes him even more effective and valued. No one likes Ted. Ted is not popular. No one trusts Ted. Ted is not human. He is Mr. Spock,

Captain Kirk's pointy-eared icon of unfeeling rationality. He has no feelings, and shows no interest in the feelings of others. But he works harder, longer, and faster than everyone else does. He is the first to arrive, and the last to leave. Being enthusiastic is not enough for Ted. He is passionate about his work, a raging passion for greatness. For most people, work gives life meaning. For Ted, work *is* life. He will pull all-nighters. Weekends. Holidays. No job is too tough. No sacrifice is too big. Whom do you call to lay off 10,000 workers, or cut the Christmas bonus? Ted. Wife and kids? You would never know he had any. Dedication? With his dying breath, Ted will whisper that he wishes he had spent more time at work.

So that in organizations driven by the bottom line, where "winning isn't everything, it's the only thing," a Ted's shortcomings as a member of the Informal Organization will be readily overlooked and excused, and, like a Bob, he can expect to receive all the hugs and kisses, all the stroking and rewards the organization has to give.

What do Carol and Ted reveal about succeeding in today's workplace? Philosophers would formalize it this way: Lack of satisfactory job performance as a member of the Formal Organization or the Informal Organization is a *necessary*, but not a *sufficient* reason to separate Dead Wood from the organization.

Survival Norm #17: "And the Oscar goes to . . . You!"
If the whole working world is a Hollywood movie starring
you and Dead Wood, then there are only three basic
story lines that are ever acted out. Those three plots are

recycled again and again in an almost infinite variety of locations, sets, scenes, and actors. Nevertheless, every tale of Dead Wood, the challenge and the response, is one of three and only three epic narratives. Decades of research and hundreds of formal studies of the have-nots versus the have-lots have only managed to isolate a single talent or personality trait that accurately predicts success and achievement in Corporate America. That is the distinct ability to picture one's working life as a heroic journey, its ups and downs as a series of adventures, culminating in final victory for its hero. There must be power in thinking positively. Be believing that you will survive the hazards and perils of your journey, and overcome the crisis of Dead Wood, and you will emerge from those assorted tests and setbacks victorious. The "Jaws" plot begins with Dead Wood doing bad things to hurt the company and his work group. You, the hero, eagerly go into battle against Dead Wood and get your ass kicked. Dead Wood continues to threaten the community with disarray and despair. You withdraw and return when you have figured out what you did wrong and what you must do to win. The final confrontation results in victory and the restoration of peace and order to the workplace. The "E.T." plot begins with an immature, inexperienced hero forced to engage Dead Wood. Dead Wood fights you again and again. Because of your shortcomings, you lose every encounter. But you emerge from each test wiser, more mature, and better prepared for the next challenge. Dead Wood forces you, the hero, to grow up again and demonstrate new leadership that ultimately brings new harmony to your work group. The third and final plot, "Close Encounters," begins with a valuable prize for which the hero goes on a hazardous journey. You will seek a solution to the problem of Dead Wood. You realize that the quest will be difficult and demanding. But you "just know" that you will find it. There is no doubt, from the get-go, that you will go the distance and you will get the prize. Only the in-betweens are uncertain. Actually, all three plots can be characterized the same way: Dead Wood is vanquished! Picture yourself overcoming Dead Wood through any one of these Spielberg films, and become the hero of your working life. We are what we pretend to be.

Eight:
Back Off! Doing the right thing:

So you're mad as hell and tired of losing sleep, and you decide to do what is right to protect the organization. (Not to mention preserving your own self-respect and professional integrity.) Go ahead, just try to fire or otherwise get rid of your Dead Wood. Then get ready for several big surprises.

First, you can't. Why? The organization won't let you.

Huh?

Unions, professional associations, federal, state, and local legalities, and your company's own HR department's rules, regulations, policies, and procedures are only the beginning of the job protections that will automatically kick-start the moment after you give notice to your employee. In fact, as a general rule, as Dead Wood's uselessness (and your blood pressure) increases, so does the number of hoops you will have to jump through to get rid of him. And the last one will be a flaming hoop.

That's because in the end the focus of everyone's attention will not be where you want it to be, that is on Dead Wood's incompetence and failings as an employee. It will instead be squarely on you, on your coaching ability, on your management style, and on your job performance as the employee's supervisor.

Did you clearly and unambiguously assign specific and measurable tasks and goals with reasonable time lines? Did you assign goals that conform to and do not exceed the employee's job description? Did you assign goals that are appropriate to the employee's skills, training, and experience? Did you assign goals that require "normal" effort, or did you require more effort from the employee compared to his peers? Did you provide the necessary human and financial resources to achieve the assigned goals and deadlines? Did you provide appropriate monitoring and adequate feedback concerning the employee's progress? Did you communicate clear warnings of weaknesses and deficiencies in the employee's job performance in a timely manner, and carefully detail the steps necessary to correct them? Finally, did you leave a paper trail that is legally unimpeachable documenting all of this to the smallest detail? You say you don't have a law degree. TS (Tough Situation). Because, any misstep, and chances are you have made plenty of "mistakes," and your HR department will be the first in line to advise against getting rid of Dead Wood. And if that isn't discouraging enough, when Dead Wood fights back by filing lawsuits and formal grievances accusing you of everything from being unfair and inept to malicious and evil, you will feel so battered and abused that you will curse yourself for ever trying to do the right thing. Before you tackle that, take a deep breath. Then take two Xanax, two Librium, drink heavily, and start smoking!

In theory, employees not protected by a labor contract can be fired without a reason. In practice, however, the courts generally will protect whistleblowers from retaliation, longtime workers for no other reason, workers who have had satisfactory performance appraisals, and workers victimized by any one of the hundreds of creative types of discrimination. A badly handled firing that cannot be defended in court is worse than none at all.

The Bottom Line: Back Off!

Second, you can't. Why? Everyone will despise you. What?

There are two competing world-views available to dealing with Dead Wood. Let's call them the Just World and the Golden WoRULEd (sounds like "world"). The Just World dictates that the productive worker shall be rewarded, and the nonproductive worker punished. In the long run, the productive worker receives a promotion, and the nonproductive worker is fired. There are only two possible mistakes that can be made in the Just World: Punish the productive worker, and reward the nonproductive worker.

The Golden WoRULEd, on the other hand, dictates that the nonproductive worker shall receive mercy, and not punishment. Reward the productive. Turn the other cheek. Reward the nonproductive, too.

Which side of the world do you think more people would choose to live on? Well, most people will say that they prefer to live in the Just World, but since no one wants to do the dirty work, most people buy property in the Golden WoRULEd. Is it really so important that the working world be a just place where the useless employee is dismissed? Is it not enough that the good employee is as rewarded as he deserves to be, and the ineffective employee is tolerated? After all, the Just World is an important theory. But an abstract theory is not more important than flesh-and-blood people with families are. People are more important than principles.

Defending one by depriving a fellow human being of his livelihood and jeopardizing his children's future feels excessive and too harsh. Is there any real harm done by showing humanity and compassion, and overlooking the useless employee?

No one ever received any credit or applause for firing anyone, no matter how useless. Expect the opposite. The Dead Wood you fire today will be a figure of sympathy and compassion tomorrow, and an object of comfort and support from everyone else. On top of being publicly stigmatized by Dead Wood and his advocates as inhumane, wicked, cruel, and uncivilized, your friends will be ashamed of you. That's one of the unacknowledged reasons why Corporate America's boards of directors rarely fire the CEO and only as a last resort, and then hand him millions of dollars he hasn't earned as he leaves the company "to spend more time with his family."

The Bottom Line: It never looks good to have your hand on the dagger. Just look at what happened to Brutus, and he was Caesar's buddy.

Third, you can't. Why? No one will back you up.

Your boss will tell you that it's your decision to make, and he will "stand behind you." (Right where you can shield him, and he will be safe from the inevitable fallout.) Your colleagues, who have been pressuring you to do something about that idiot on your staff, will deny that they ever encouraged you to fire him. His clients will admit that they complained about him, sure, but say they never meant to suggest that you should fire him. His co-workers and peers, even those who griped the most about him, and those who suffered the most by having to work harder because of him, will take cover and deny that they know any reason you would have to fire him. So what if your decision was more about him not serving his clients and not carrying his weight with his co-workers than it was about you being true to your own standards and professionalism. So what if you fired him more for the benefit of their morale and job satisfaction than your own. Do not expect a pat on the back from them. Do expect them to turn their backs on you. You will be all alone.

The Bottom Line: Many will be called, but few will not choose to turn their back on you.

Fourth, you can't. Why? Dead Wood is too popular.

One of the nastiest surprises that will hit you when attempting to get rid of Dead Wood is how many loyal and intensely devoted supporters and advocates will suddenly appear out of thin air who can't wait to confront you and stick up for him. How fiercely they will rally to the defense of Dead Wood, asserting his value to the company and celebrating his accomplishments, like an eagle protecting its nest. At first, you will feel confused, believing for a moment that they are describing someone else. You will feel obligated to pay attention to long, glowing testimonials to Dead Wood's inner goodness and character, and dissertations filled with Dead Wood's unique and indispensable contributions which (they say) have been instrumental in making the company the great success it is today. The whole time, you will be wondering what they have been drinking that they cannot see Dead Wood's serious weaknesses, deficiencies, and failings as clearly as you see them. How can so many of your otherwise sensible and intelligent colleagues believe that

Dead Wood is an asset to the company, and not a useless and unnecessary drag on the payroll?

How? Dead Wood is very much in the eye of the beholder. Even the least of employees, no matter how useless and unnecessary, and no matter how many teammates and co-workers do not like him, will have a large network of loyal friends and supporters standing by him in the organization. Dead Wood isn't Dead Wood to Dead Wood.

The Bottom Line: Don't be deceived by what people say. Everyone always preaches against Dead Wood. Everyone always agrees that the company ought to clean house and get rid of it. Until you try. Then they find a rope and a tree, and come looking for you. Because one man's Dead Wood is another man's supreme being.

Survival Norm #18: Use Balance Theory to Win Friends and Get Rid of People!

Wouldn't it be nice to foresee whether or not you will like someone and whether that person will like you before you know anything more about each other or even meet face-to-face for the first time? Wouldn't it be nice to be able to forecast which personal friendships and political alliances will form between which members of the same work group? Wouldn't it be nice to know beforehand which potential social relationships will turn out to be positive and which ones will turn sour and negative, so you can decide where to build bridges and where to burn them? Nice? A crystal ball that can predict positive and negative relationships between people, including you, would be the greatest invention since glow-in-the-dark condoms! Well, turn off the lights, because

*it's here, it works, and it is known as Balance Theory.
Balance Theory states that all social relationships involving
three persons or triads are driven toward emotional
balance. To be emotionally in balance, the liking and
disliking feelings and attitudes that characterize these three
relationships must multiply out to a positive result. Consider
the triadic relationship between you, Dead Wood, and Fire
Wood. Because you dislike Dead Wood and Dead Wood
dislikes you, the relationship is negative. Now suppose
Dead Wood and Fire Wood like each other and become
friends, and that relationship is positive. If you should try,
and you should, to build a positive, liking relationship with
Fire Wood, you will fail, because then the triad will multiply
out to a negative result and be emotionally unbalanced. (A
negative times a positive times a positive equals a negative,
triadic imbalance.) People will always avoid an imbalance,
and when he perceives an emotional imbalance, the person
will resolve the dilemma and satisfy the drive in a way that
requires the least amount of effort. The problem is that
by being the first one to establish a positive relationship
with Fire Wood, Dead Wood has driven him toward feeling
negatively about you in order to maintain the necessary
psychological balance. (A negative times a negative times a
positive equals a positive, emotionally balanced triad.) That
means Dead Wood wins a loyal supporter and advocate,
and you lose Luke to Darth Vader and The Dark Side. If
you had created a positive relationship with Fire Wood, then
he would be driven toward negative feelings about Dead
Wood. Now you are left with several bad options. You
can decide that Fire Wood isn't as great as you originally
thought and accept your lousy relationship with him. You
can try to force Fire Wood to "switch sides". (A do-over*

that worked well with Judas!) Or, you can decide that Dead Wood isn't so bad after all. Then you can pursue a positive relationship with Fire Wood that will keep the triad in balance. (A positive times a positive times a positive equals a positive.) The solution is to use Balance Theory to predict the outcome of a triad. First, you must recruit and otherwise screen-in to your triads Fire Wood that has already formed or can be motivated to form positive feelings about you. Then, Balance Theory predicts that he will dislike Dead Wood and turn against him to protect the balance. (The enemy of my enemy is my friend.) Second, Balance Theory dictates that it is extremely difficult and unlikely you will ever be able to overcome the psychological and emotional harmony produced as a result of a negative relationship with Fire Wood. Therefore, if his friendship with Dead Wood is deeper and stronger than his bond with you, then to satisfy the drive toward balance and steer the triad away from becoming out of balance, your relationship with Fire Wood is bound to crash and burn. It's not up to him and it's not about you. It's Balance: The enemy of my friend is my enemy. So, your best option is to evict him from the triad, and from now on, when you build your networks and pick your friends, use Balance Theory.

Fifth, you can't. Why? The "Halo Effect" protects Dead Wood.

Unless you founded or helped start the company, you are an employee because someone else in the company hired you. And it is very important for you and your future how highly regarded that other employee is, and how much face and standing does he have in the company. If he is a towering figure in the organization with enormous personal and position power, then the great charisma and authority possessed by him becomes a symbolic halo around his head. And by becoming your champion and endorsing your talent and potential, you have a halo symbolically placed around your head. It does not have the same meaning as the one he wears which is due to his impressive status and influence. Your halo means that you have received his seal of approval. For example, on your first day at Microsoft, your new colleagues defer to you with awe and respect, "He must be special. Why? Bill Gates himself hired him." That's the Halo Effect at work at work.

So what happens when Dear Leader, the great and powerful, hires the wrong person and adds more Dead Wood to the organization? Then the Halo Effect becomes an effective deterrent to ever getting rid of the useless. Challenging the CEO's wisdom, experience, and judgment by attacking the competence of someone he has already blessed would be politically incorrect, to put it mildly. Even the CEO cannot question his own opinion and once it has been bestowed, revoke his blessing. Because that would be the same as admit he made a king-sized mistake in the first place. And that goes for all the other big shots at the top of the chain of command that bulletproof their own Dead Wood to avoid losing face as well. And so, the Halo Effect becomes permanent, and getting rid of Dead Wood is more complicated than ever. For example, after five troubled years on the job, your colleagues at Microsoft snicker behind your back, "He's an idiot. But we're stuck with him. Why? He was hired by Bill Gates himself." That's also the Halo Effect.

Furthermore, that is by no means the only way of earning a halo. Other haloes produce the same dysfunctional consequences. Persistence engenders a special halo. For example, "He's an idiot. But we're stuck with him. Why? He's been with the company for 25 years." "Why? He's retiring in two years." "Why? He turns 62 in five years." Personal hardships produce another kind of halo. For example, "He's an idiot. But we're stuck with him. Why? He's putting his two kids through college." "Why? He is a recovering alcoholic." "Why? He and his wife are getting divorced." "Why? SIDS Baby."

School and fraternity ties are immensely powerful haloes in the business world. Hiring decisions based on loyalty to educational institutions and longing for one's past breed Dead Wood faster than you can jump up and shout, "Go Bulldogs!" and undermine the organization's mission to build and protect meritocracies.

The Bottom Line: Haloes of all kinds make it more difficult and unpopular to get rid of Dead Wood, and therefore more unlikely.

So, you think the company will greet you with cheers for cleaning out its Dead Wood. Think again! Your best friends will run away and you will wind up nailed to a cross between two other nuts, while Dead Wood will have more allies and more job security than ever.

Survival Norm #19: You Need To Be A Mentor!
If Dead Wood has one defining, essential characteristic, it is that he does not want to be bossed. But you already know that does not work. Dead Wood hates bureaucracy.

*Dead Wood does not recognize the corporate hierarchy
of power and authority. And Dead Wood has no respect
for traditional managers who try to order him around as
if he is the same as everyone else under your supervision.
Remember, these employees feel that they are different and
don't need you. So, the problem is how do you manage your
a**holes? The solution is by acting more like a guardian
angel and a lot less like a traditional boss. Listen carefully
to how Dead Wood says he deserves to be treated. Make
a point of talking extensively with Dead Wood to find out
what he really wants and needs from you. Schedule your
time together, setting aside, say, an hour a day to start with,
exclusively for Dead Wood. When he puffs up and becomes
overly chatty, ask scores of questions and do plenty of
listening. Boil down everything that Dead Wood has to
say, and his theme will be that he feels over-managed. You
would say that he is under-managed. The truth is that he is
being mismanaged. Dead Wood will tell you that he wants
more freedom – freedom to ignore, freedom to dabble, and
freedom to disappoint. Whatever he wants, you give it to
him, whether it's a special deal, a one-time accommodation,
or a permanent exemption from this or that rule or
obligation! Just don't forget to get what you need in
return! A mentor is not a pal, a mom, or a cheerleader.
A mentor is someone whose only role is to tell the truth,
the whole truth, and nothing but the truth. That's their
real value. Tell him what you want from him. Talk about
specific issues. Establish specific goals and expectations.
Tell him about your sore spots and his weak spots. Give
him advice that will help strengthen his skills, but don't be
a dictator. Keep your advice objective, but don't sugarcoat
it. Be his confidant, but don't get too close and don't let*

the relationship become too personal. Mentoring is strictly business, so keep personal problems out of the discussion. If you can establish the right chemistry, the payoff will be big. Paul had John. John had Yoko. Things didn't always go smoothly. But a good mentor can bring out the best and remediate the worst in almost anyone, especially Dead Wood.

Nine:
Speaking in tongues:
The logicalization of Dead Wood:

So you've finally pulled yourself together and managed to summon up your righteous anger and fortify your integrity, marshaled a boatload of verifiable facts and circumstances, and are ready to hold Dead Wood accountable for his inadequacies and failings. How do you expect Dead Wood will respond to your criticisms so as to justify himself? Justification, you ask? Impossible! Besides, you have indisputable proof that he is lazy and stupid. How can he possibly defend himself? No way!

Not so fast! Dead Wood will have plenty of tales to tell that devise plausible explanations of his "failings" and demonstrate how they actually add great value to the organization. In the alternate universe where Dead Wood works, that you have only seen in reruns of the old "Star Trek" television program, his job performance is more than defensible. By the end, using equally solid, but competing facts, and the same cold geometric logic, he will prove that he is one of your best workers, that he is underrated and underappreciated, and that if you're not satisfied with his work, it's your fault!

Let's go through briefly several of the more cunning and clever arguments you should be prepared to hear from Dead Wood, in these or like-minded words.

The Mindreader
"I have always done everything you asked me to do. If you have not told me what you want me to do, then

it is not fair of you to criticize me now for not having done it. How am I supposed to know what you expect of me, if you don't tell me? Do I look like I have the power to read minds? Have you seen a crystal ball in my office? If you want me to work harder and do better, all you have to do is let me know, and I will. That's your job, isn't it? If you don't do your job, then I can't be expected to do mine. It's not fair to blame me for your negligence. I can only do what you tell me. If that is not enough, then you are as much to blame as I am. It's your fault!"

The Miracle Worker

"Your standards and expectations are too high. You require too much of me. I am only human. I can't do more or better than I already am. Everyone has his limits. I can only do so much. I can't give you what is impossible for me to give. And it is wrong for you to demand that I do. Am I supposed to do the impossible? Do you expect me to be able to work miracles? You're asking me to walk on water! That's not fair! No one can do what you are requiring of me. My last boss was fair, so he was always happy with my work. You are to blame, not me. Your standards are unreasonable and unfair. You expect too much. Everyone else thinks so, too. It's your fault!"

The Scapegoat

"You have never liked me. You are constantly criticizing me. Everyone else makes the same mistakes as I do, but I am the only one you pick on. It is because I'm different, isn't it? It is because I'm blonde, isn't it? It is because I'm a woman, isn't it? It is because I'm short, isn't it? It is because I'm gay, isn't it? What do you have against people like me? You never blame so-and-so for anything. That's favoritism! You're prejudiced against my kind. That's Discrimination! That's wrong! It's your fault!"

The Philosopher

"What do you mean, my work is not good enough? I am working as hard as I can. I am doing the best that I can. I am as busy and productive as I can possibly be. Why isn't that good enough for you? Do you expect me to do better than my best? That's crazy and illogical! You're talking nonsense. How can I do better when I am already doing my best? Better is better than good and best is better than better. Therefore, my best is better than your good. If you were more logical, my best would be more than enough to satisfy you. Why are you being so irrational? Since you can plainly see that I am already doing my best, it is absurd for you to demand more than that. You're not making sense. That's unfair! It's your fault!"

The Referee

"My work is not good enough? I work just as long and hard as most other people in the company. There may be a handful of fanatics who do more than I do. But what about him? *His* work sucks. And her? *She* is lazier and makes many more mistakes than I do. There are plenty of others doing a lot worse than I am. So what are you doing about *them?* How can my work be that bad? Nothing is bad if 100 people are doing it. Blame 99 of them. Don't blame me. I don't set standards, I just obey them. You're in charge. You make the rules. If you don't like them, then it's your responsibility to change them. Then everyone will work harder, me included. You're not doing your job! It's your fault!"

The Bottom Line: Before you ask, the answer is an unequivocal Yes: Dead Wood knows that it is Dead Wood. Nevertheless, Dead Wood never accepts responsibility for being Dead Wood. Prepare yourself! They may be lazy and stupid in all other respects, but Dead Wood plays "the blame game" like a chess grandmaster, tirelessly calculating many moves ahead. Winning means escaping accountability by shifting the blame to you.

Survival Norm #20: Better to Don't Do the Don'ts than to Do the Do's!
Many of my prescriptive and proscriptive norms for surviving and making the most of Dead Wood are valuable tools for dealing with several other important types of employees, both good and bad, and other types of

situations, both functional and dysfunctional. However, a handful of Do Not as opposed to Do rules don't cut across managerial lines because they are peculiar to Dead Wood, and therefore, are deserving of special recognition in our toolbox. One, don't try to create a Garden of Eden. You can't change Dead Wood into a different kind of person, no one can. But you can influence and change his way of thinking, feeling, and acting. And there is nothing inherently wrong with trying to influence his behavior by meeting his needs and enhancing his work environment in order to win his trust, confidence, and good will. But you need to know where to draw the line between personal and professional needs. And the line between kissing-up and kissing-off is easy to move. Move it the wrong way, and you will burn out long before he is fully appeased. Two, don't mismanage your emotional distance. Know where to draw the line between becoming too personal and too emotional and becoming too professional and too cool and distant. Too professional, and you give up the pal or buddy influence. Too personal, and you give up the impact of a boss or colleague. Three, don't be the one to tell Dead Wood that he's doing something wrong. Dead Wood is very defensive and overly sensitive to criticism, so don't damage your relationship. Figure out who else Dead Wood respects and confides in, and use that person as a conduit for your complaints and criticism. That person will carry your disappointment to Dead Wood, and you won't have to do the dirty work. Four, don't make him look bad, help him look good. Dead Wood is highly susceptible to flattery and buttering up. Celebrity is our culture's heroin. Get him hooked, and he will sell his sister, and most anything else you ask of him, he'll do, just to maintain his connection. Five, don't lose hope. This is most important. Dead Wood is one of the few workplace demons that can drive good, otherwise conscientious employees to shrug and look the other way. But if you give up, then he wins, and you become part of the problem. Then someone like me will have to write a book about what to do with people like you.

Ten:
Walk toward the light:
Positive functions of Dead Wood:

Looked at another way, Dead Wood can be helpful as well as hurtful to the organization and its Fire Wood. The stubborn, weed-like persistence of Dead Wood, and the Sisyphean, uphill struggle required to get rid of it, are the direct result of these positive and beneficial functions. So an understanding of that cause-and-effect relationship may be more than interesting and enlightening. It may suggest some creative tools and techniques that we can take advantage of down the road to better manage and exploit Dead Wood for the good of the organization.

One of the most important of these positive functions of Dead Wood is to maintain, protect, and enhance everyone else's job security. As long as Dead Wood is on the payroll, Fire Wood can feel more confident that its place in the organization is safe and secure. By assuming correctly that if downsizing becomes necessary, the rational organization will always choose to unload its useless Dead Wood before its valuable Fire Wood. Dead Wood provides an unwritten and unintended but no less effective type of job protection for Fire Wood. Therefore, it is to Fire Wood's advantage to keep some Dead Wood on the payroll, and not to eliminate all Dead Wood. As a matter of fact, the best Dead Wood to retain in the organization turns out to be the very deadest of the Dead Wood. The worst of the worst employees make the best security blanket. That's because the more inequality that exists between Dead Wood and Fire

Wood, the less risk there is to Fire Wood's job security: "I am safe as long as Dead Wood is on the payroll." And greater security tends to boost job satisfaction and morale among good and marginal performers.

Employment security is a powerful incentive, especially in rapidly changing and unpredictable times. So Fire Wood becomes a stumbling block to keeping Dead Wood out of the organization, and little help in getting rid of it. You didn't expect that from Fire Wood. But it happens all the time, at all levels. Workers who are otherwise dedicated and professional deliberately add Dead Wood to the work force, and then protect it, just to make their job performance look better and feel more secure.

Second, in sociological circles, it has long been a truism that the best way to teach and reinforce the importance of conformity in a social group is to make an example of one of its offenders, as in public lynching in the late 1700's. In modern work groups, Dead Wood plays that all-important social role, and is maintained and protected as a member of the organization to perform that all-important function. When Fire Wood needs to demonstrate the penalties of poor performance, Dead Wood makes an ideal candidate for a symbolic lynching. When fault-finders need a target for their scorn and ridicule, Dead Wood is handy to keep nearby. When something goes terribly wrong, and blame has to be placed on someone, Dead Wood can be put to good use.

In general, desirable traits and habits are easier to teach and learn where undesirable ones are available for retaliation and punishment. The more undisciplined and untrained a team of workers is, the more valuable and necessary Dead Wood becomes to management as a motivational device. Because responding to Dead Wood affirms team values and norms, promotes group solidarity and social unity, and clarifies moral and ethical boundaries. When you squash an anthill under your foot and then watch the ants, they suddenly look a lot more energetic and motivated, don't they?

Third, when downsizing and restructuring become necessary for sound management reasons, and one or more team members must be let go, Dead Wood functions as a ready-made pool of unemployables and fall guys. That way, management can control the size of its work force without undermining overall productivity and organizational success, which, ideally, should remain almost unchanged. Labor costs go down. Profits go up. And management looks good in a crisis. The key to that strategy is maintaining and protecting Dead Wood on the payroll in anticipation of right-sizing in tough times.

Fourth, downsizing and upsizing have become facts of life in Corporate America. However, in those organizations that are rebranding and permanently repositioning in the marketplace, or permanently streamlining the internal decision-making process, downsizing can mean permanent Reduction In Force. And RIF is another one of those weird situations where it makes more sense to nurture and protect Dead Wood on the payroll than get rid of it. That sounds backwards, doesn't it? RIF ought to be one of the best chances and golden opportunities to rid the organization easily and permanently of Dead Wood. But protecting Dead Wood during RIF can be a perfectly rational management decision. For even a "heartbeat" is better than a vacant position that is permanently eliminated and lost forever. "Headcount is better than no count."

As a rule, in most HR departments, how highly rewarded a manager should be, as well as the reach of his influence and status in the organization, are positively correlated with "headcount," meaning, the size of his support staff and number of direct reports. Size matters. Bigger is better. Keeping Dead Wood on the payroll also keeps the position on the organizational chart until it can be filled with a better performer. Managers can often be seen fighting to keep one of their worst employees on the payroll, because the position is more important than the person is, and a warm body is better than nobody.

Finally, let's conduct a thought-experiment. Imagine that Fire Wood is planning to request a salary increase for himself, and needs to provide a solid justification to support his request. Now imagine that another member of his peer group is in the same job as Fire Wood, with the same responsibilities and assignments, and equal in pay. Now suppose that Fire Wood's teammate is Dead Wood. Fire Wood will support his request by arguing that because he is doing the same job as Dead Wood, but much more competently and productively, his salary should be adjusted higher. That's an argument difficult to dispute and easy to win.

Every team values its Dead Wood and clings to it for that reason. When job performance has to be compared, evaluated, and rewarded, Dead Wood means money in Fire Wood's pocket. Dead Wood may not be easy to get rid of, but why would anyone even try? The numbest of skulls – unrestrained by fear of failure, disapproval, or looking foolish – sets the standard.

The Bottom Line: Dead Wood has its rightful place in the organization. It can serve a useful purpose, and perform several positive and important latent functions. Therefore, Dead Wood may be synonymous with Good-For-Nothing, but Dead Wood is by no means good for nothing.

Survival Norm #21: Think Outside Your Box, Think Inside His Box!

People who belong to tight, solid, cohesive social networks, whether in the same office, company, industry, or profession, may be happier living in a homogeneous social world where everyone you know is like you. But people who cling to their own social group will have a lot more difficulty finding new ideas and innovative solutions to the many organizational and interpersonal troubles caused by Dead Wood. That's because people in the same network tend to think, feel, and act the same. They share the same creativity and imagination as well as the same ways of critical thinking and problem solving. That's what united them in the first place, isn't it? As a result, if you ask your network for advice, the only help they will be able to give you are the same moldy, overworked, moth-eaten ideas you already had that didn't work when you tried them. The solution to the problem of finding new solutions is to reach outside your immediate group and inside other kinds of work groups with similar problems. Think outside your box, and inside a different box. You will discover ideas that may be well known and mundane in another group that are novel and valuable in your group. If you are an architect, then find out how construction workers and hard hats handle Dead Wood. If you are a banker, then find out how hair stylists deal with Dead Wood in the salon. If you are in advertising, then ask an auto mechanic for advice. Contact people outside your social orbit. Ask about Dead Wood. They too have their story. To be more creative and find good ideas, look for people who are completely ignorant about what you do, and learn how they solve your problems for themselves. Good ideas are not born, they are transplanted.

Eleven:
Beware of the dark side:
Negative functions of Dead Wood:

Every one of your competitors has the same buildings and the same technology as you do. They have the same policies and procedures, and the same strategic plans and priorities. These are commodities. The only leverageable asset in today's world of work is imagination or creativity or the potential to generate new ideas.

All new ideas enter the world through the mind of one man. You wouldn't be reading this book if Johannes Gutenberg hadn't invented movable type in the 1440s. And if John Logie Baird hadn't discovered a way to televise moving pictures in the 1920s, you would not be able to watch Steve Guttenberg after midnight in all those dumb "Police Academy" films. Just as there is no such thing as a collective mind, committees are incapable of creativity and invention. "Two heads are better than one." Whatever man or woman first said that, it's false. Two heads or a thousand can do no better than one, and usually a lot worse. I challenge you to name a single instance where a group produced a genuinely creative idea. What people call "brainstorming" should be called "cobabblation." That's why, it is wisely said, "A camel is a horse designed by a committee."

Therefore, over time, the most damaging impact of Dead Wood's stubborn persistence and unforgivable prosperity is to thoroughly undermine the organization's culture of meritocracy, otherwise known as pay for performance. And that cultural ideal is the chief cornerstone of the organization's ability to successfully recruit and retain its supply of creative Fire Wood. Since Fire Wood is the key to differentiating organizations from their competitors in the marketplace, Dead Wood not only jeopardizes organizational success now, but longer-term, the organization's survivability. Let's give that negative function a familiar name. Call it Gresham's Law of Human Capital, "Dead Wood drives out Fire Wood."

You hear it all the time. Standards are falling everywhere in society. And as standards decline, there tends to be a coarsening of human behavior as well. Why? Because people will achieve whichever standard is set for them, but will reach no higher. People will rise to challenges and meet expectations, but will not exceed them. Set a high standard, and most people will be high achievers. Set a low standard, and most people will be underachievers. That's why, it is always easier to lower standards than it is to raise them. In his best book, "On Aggression" (1963), Konrad Lorenz, the Nobel prize-winning ethologist, famously observed that microscopic organisms are lazy, and exhibit locomotion only when they experience pain or discomfort, like couch potatoes with a full bladder. Most people will work no harder than they are required, and will work as little as they can get away with. Therefore, as a rule of thumb, in life as in work, set higher standards at first, and then lower them deliberately and for good reason, always mindful that it will be almost impossible to raise them back up again.

That's the second major problem caused by Dead Wood. Dead Wood constantly pressures performance standards, revising them downward for everyone else on the same team or in the same work group. If a rising tide lifts all boats, then you can guess what happens when the tide is falling. What was once poor performance becomes fair, fair becomes good, good becomes excellent, and everyone except long-timers who reminisce about "the good old days" quickly forgets the true meaning of excellence. And "Good Work!" eventually means anything that most people can be persuaded to believe it is.

Frederick Taylor, the father of scientific management, who led America's obsession with efficiency in the early 20th century, wrote, "When a naturally energetic man works for a few days beside a lazy one, the logic of the situation is unanswerable. 'Why should I work hard when that lazy fellow gets the same pay I do and does only half the work?' "

The third problem is like the second, and just as insidious. But in addition to undermining standards, Dead Wood exerts downward pressure on his colleagues' job satisfaction and employee morale. Can you imagine how it feels to be Fire Wood working day after day on the same team, side-by-side with Dead Wood? You are hard working and productive. Dead Wood is lazy and stupid. You successfully complete your fair share of the workload assigned to the team. Dead Wood does not carry his own weight, and you have to help carry it for him. *Because* of you, the team is a success. *Despite* Dead Wood, the team is a success. At the end of the day, you earn a certain salary and other rewards, and benefit from the team's positive reputation and reflected glory. To the last penny, Dead Wood receives the same tangible rewards as you do, and shares the same respect and recognition as you or any other team member.

Making matters worse, Dead Wood is a sin against one of society's deepest and most cherished beliefs, the fair or just world. Ideally, good workers are supposed to be rewarded, and incompetent workers punished. But Fire Wood feels that he is working more and rewarded less than he should be, because Dead Wood is working less and rewarded more than he should be. Why do good things happen to bad workers and bad things happen to good workers? In a just world, that is unfair and demoralizing.

The emotional impact on Fire Wood of being Dead Wood's teammate is bound to be extremely negative. Dead Wood has a way of cloning himself by making everyone he touches less committed and more uncaring and disengaged. Fire Wood's dedication and drive inevitably grow weaker. On Friday, he is bitter and depressed about having to return to work on Monday. And on Monday, he is bitter and depressed about how many more days there are until Friday. One fine day, like always, he takes a coffee break, and like Edwin Arlington Robinson's Richard Cory, he never returns. Longer-term, he becomes a relentless clock-watcher, a 9-to-5 humdrum worker, doing his job by the numbers, just to collect a paycheck, but without passion or caring, and never going beyond Dead Wood's "normal" effort. As Fire Wood's attitude and job performance continue to deteriorate, he becomes more and more like Dead Wood. In time, he will be.

Survival Norm #22: Embrace Your Inner Caveman

*If you could simply ax dysfunctional workers, you wouldn't
need me to help you get the better of a bad situation.
And other readers wouldn't be snapping up copies of like-
minded books that address the boss as bully, the weirdo
subordinate, the team of oddballs, and other problem
personalities. So why not just eliminate them and detoxify
your work environment? You don't need a Harvard
professor to tell you that companies that get rid of their
bad apples are more productive and profitable than those
that tolerate and cater to them. The problem is that you
are afraid to fire problem workers. And you are in great
and growing company. Those other readers have the same
fear of firing. And it's the worst kind of fear … rational
fear! On April 23, 2007, "Business Week's" Cover Story
reported that companies are so terrified of lawsuits, unions,
as well as their own lawyers and HR departments that
they let screwups screw up, lay off productive workers while
retaining unproductive workers, and pay severance (read:
bribery) to goof-offs so they won't sue. Fear of firing has
created a protected class of unproductive untouchables that
demotivates everyone else, and revises workforce quality
downward. The solution is to obey your fear. The world
has evolved, but human nature has not. We look different,
but our survival instincts are the same as they ever were.
The way in which we are programmed to make decisions,
especially in dangerous situations, is the very same way our
primitive ancestors made them. We run away first and ask
questions later. The cavemen who didn't obey their fear,
who didn't run from imminent danger, who studied the
threat, who analyzed and evaluated the situation coldly and
rationally, didn't pass on their decision-making genes to us.*

That's because they didn't survive. Harvard Business School tells us to fire Dead Wood. But the caveman within tells us to avoid risk, run first, then evaluate the situation. The solution is so simple even a caveman can do it. Listen to eggheads instead of your inner caveman and you will stray too far from the herd, where Dead Wood will make a meal of you.

Looked at from Dead Wood's otherworldly perspective, nothing succeeds like failure. It turns out that there is not much of a downside to stupidity, and a considerable upside. Management looks at Dead Wood and sees poor work habits, low energy, weak or incomplete skills, and lack of enthusiasm and commitment. Management looks at Fire Wood and sees the right stuff. So knee-jerk management, aiming above all to get the work done as well as it can be done, assigns less work to Dead Wood and delegates more work to Fire Wood. Likewise, the more rigorous and demanding the job and the more important it is to management that the job be well done, the more likely it is to be delegated to Fire Wood. It doesn't take long for Dead Wood to figure out that the more incompetently and ineffectively he performs, and the more shoddy his work becomes, the more aggressively management tends to reassign more of the team's workload as well as the more difficult and demanding jobs to Fire Wood. That leaves Dead Wood with less work to do, the easier, least stressful jobs included.

The mistakes are taught in Management 101, just waiting to be made. In the MBA classroom, future managers are brainwashed like North Koreans to believe that to be successful their primary mission must always be to motivate their subordinates to do their jobs as well as managers know they can be done if managers did the jobs themselves. (That is how we of the Ivory Tower are either molding the leaders of tomorrow, or more likely, leading the mold of tomorrow.) Therefore, in the real-life world, where most textbook theories usually have little applicability, these apple-polishers prefer to strip away assignments and responsibilities that do not fit a worker's talents and interests, and reassign those duties to more able, more qualified co-workers. Dead Wood forfeits the tough jobs to other team members, "dumbing-down" his role on the team to the lightest workload, easier jobs, and lowest expectations. In other words, textbook management plays directly into the hands of Dead Wood.

Failure amounts to an altogether rational career choice for Dead Wood. Because failure leads to less work, less responsibility, less accountability, and less stress, and to more leisure time and attention to build political capital by strengthening one's relationships, alliances, and networks in the Informal Organization. Thanks to management, Dead Wood, up to now unofficially unproductive but at least busy, is now officially both idle and more unproductive than ever. Meanwhile, Fire Wood has more work and more responsibility piled on it, is under more pressure and is more stressed-out than ever.

Fire Wood or Dead Wood? Assuming both jobs receive about equal pay, which one would you rather do? Fire Wood makes his job bigger and more important than the way he found it. Dead Wood trivializes his job description and makes it a lot smaller and less important than it once was. Fire Wood expands his "turf" by taking on more work, more responsibility, and more authority, and leaves it richer and more diverse than before he was put in charge of it. Dead Wood burns fewer calories doing his job than his predecessor did. Fire Wood found his job half-full and filled it to overflowing. Dead Wood found his job half-empty and poked a hole in the bottom.

Good workers can make bad jobs good.

Bad workers can make good jobs bad.

Hypothetically, let's say that Fire Wood receives greater intangible "pay" than Dead Wood in the form of more respect and recognition from one's peers, better job prospects and career mobility, as well as more emotional and even spiritual satisfaction. Then the central question becomes, "Is Fire Wood better off than Dead Wood?" The Bottom Line: Are those intangible rewards great enough to offset the big differences in workload, pressure, stress, morale, and overall satisfaction with the quality of one's professional life? If your answer is an emphatic "Hell No!" or a sarcastic "Yeah, Right!", then don't be surprised to find that bad workers drive off good workers.

Survival Norm #23: Lighten Up!

Granted, Dead Wood offends you, screws-up your team, plunders the bottom line, and gives the word paycheck a bad name. Granted, modifying or at least mollifying Dead Wood's negative behavior is more than a personal cause. It has become an all-important business result. Nevertheless, you must learn to lighten up, and help others in the office afflicted by Dead Wood to be cool, don't lose perspective, and by all means, don't forfeit one's sense of humor. The solution is to take action without taking action, to fight back without starting fights. At meetings, instead of being overly aggressive and steamrolling Dead Wood, humble yourself and ask for his opinion. Instead of shutting him down, show people that you are committed to improving and integrating Dead Wood. That's an efficient and effective way of asking for their help and commitment, without asking. Converting Dead Wood doesn't have to be a one-man show. When Dead Wood disagrees with you in front of other people, don't say "No," "But," or "Huh?" Hold the sarcasm. Don't argue with him. Instead, smile and steer. Smile, thank him for his ideas, and ask him to explain, to go into more detail and help you better understand what he means. Then, steer. Say something like this, "Thank you for your thoughts. I do like some of your ideas. This is what I am thinking (that agrees with what you said). And what I am also thinking is that we should try this (that you disagreed with)." Steering means getting Dead Wood on the same train as you are. He may not like every stop. But once he is on board, he's going to the end of the line. Bulldozing Dead Wood and crushing his ideas, no matter how contrary, is not the way to win. That is not only undignified, it disrespects Dead Wood and fuels the problem. Do you remember Aesop's fable of the sun, the wind, and the man in the overcoat? To win, you, too, must lighten up, and like the sun, master the art of fighting without fighting. Your smile and warmth can be your strongest shield and sharpest sword.

Twelve:
From Dead Wood to Fire Wood: Ten commandments that do not require chair-throwing, hair-tearing, or gunplay:

For a great many valid reasons that you have now seen and we have discussed, being on the same team with Dead Wood as a colleague or co-worker makes you feel as if Captain Hook is masturbating you. In moments of raging frustration, you want to scream, "Stop Helping Me!" Add a zillion zero's to 1, and it still adds up to just 1. The only difference is now you have lots of unwanted zero's interfering with you, blocking your way, and tying you down. It's the same feeling you get driving your car over seven or eight speedbumps in a row. Thanks to Dead Wood, it's not just a job anymore, it's an adventure!

The primary challenge to management is that Dead Wood has ceased to think like an "employee," and instead sees himself essentially as an "independent contractor." Managing Dead Wood is therefore much like managing an all-volunteer work force. You don't need to be told that the normal motivational devices that are so completely effective with Fire Wood, such as rules and regulations, hierarchy of authority, division of labor, pay-for-performance and the meritocracy, do not work well with Dead Wood. Because anyone who has worked above or below or in the general vicinity of Dead Wood on the organizational chart has already learned this the hard way from bitter experience.

That's where these ten commandments for managing Dead Wood more effectively will come in handy for almost anyone anywhere in the chain of command who wants more tools and needs better techniques for dealing with the helpless, the hapless, and the hopeless. Caveat emptor! Do not expect them to be mutually consistent or compatible or even to agree with each other. Circumstances vary wildly, as do the solutions that correlate with them. Nevertheless, at the very least, they will help restore your peace of mind, if not show you more than one right way to heal your troubled workplace.

I. Thou shalt cling and wait.

No, that's not a misprint. Everyone else you work with knows that your company has its quota of Dead Wood, and also knows where most of it is. Everyone else has his own share of Dead Wood with its negative, dysfunctional consequences and also is struggling to adapt and cope. Everyone else feels just as desperate and demoralized as you do. Everyone else has Dead Wood that cannot be fired and that they also cannot escape. Job has plenty of company in the Bible. Look harder, and you'll find that you are by no means alone. Therefore, few of your colleagues will judge you, and no one will blame you if you cut your losses, toss in the towel, and do nothing about your Dead Wood but grin and bear it. Instead, focus your efforts on exploiting the positive functions of Dead Wood. That does NOT mean you have to reconcile yourself to spend 90% of your most valuable time and attention on the useless 10% of the organization's employees who deserve a lot less, and 10% of your time and attention on the useful 90% who deserve a lot more. Be honest. Isn't that the only "solution" you've been pursuing up to now? Blame society. Because of our shared values and culture, American society favors action over reflection, so you never considered giving up to be a legitimate strategy, more of a default option than a deliberate choice. It's about time you carefully analyzed and assessed your situation objectively and dispassionately. If it is hopeless, really hopeless, then the most rational and promising approach available to you may be to sit on your hands and do nothing more to rectify the situation. The alternative is to keep doing the same things you've been doing and expect a different result, what Freud defined as insanity. Stop Reading Now! Throw this book away. And buy one on how to recognize and more effectively reward and appreciate your good employees. Cling to hope, and wait for the situation to work itself out, for where there is hope, there is life after Dead Wood. One of the best-kept secrets of the study of modern medicine is how medical school students are taught that as practicing physicians, even if they do nothing at all, 90% of the time their patients will get better all by themselves. It is not our world yet. It may give us a great deal of emotional and spiritual satisfaction to believe that things don't just get better, we have to do something to make them better, but so does believing in Santa Claus and the Easter Bunny. Human behavior has not been solved, and may never be. Even if you keep your hands off, people may get better by themselves. Patience! Everything changes, Dead Wood and Fire Wood included. There are no permanent circumstances, only permanent interests. People do so many wrong things in social relationships because they are convinced it's right. *Lack* of communication is key to a successful marriage, but most people think it's no good, even though there's plenty of evidence for it. Choose to turn a blind eye to Dead Wood. Play dumb. It is not like watching dry paint. It is not doing nothing. It is one hand clapping. It is watching paint dry. (Wink-wink, nudge-nudge.) Trust in the power of things unseen and unknown, and have faith that everything will be unfolding in your favor.

11. Thou shalt fit the job to the person.

Apologies to Nietzsche, but think of Dead Wood as a dung that must be spread thin so that a little Fire Wood can grow. The working world is a pyramid. In order to produce a few outstanding performers at the top of the pyramid, it is necessary to have a great many bottom-feeders at the base of the pyramid. Everyone is adept at doing something, and today's large, complex, bureaucratic work organization has a suitable but as yet uncreated home for its Dead Wood. Everyone, Dead Wood included, longs to feel useful and necessary, and to be perceived as an important and valued team player by his peers and significant others. Everyone needs to belong and to identify his personal interests with the goals and interests of his work group. In other words, Dead Wood are people, too. Once upon a time, Dead Wood may have filled a functionally important position in the organization. But Dead Wood's job is now trivial and useless and places an unnecessary drag on the payroll. You can't get rid of the person, so get rid of the position. Reorganize. Design a new position for Dead Wood. Do not ground that new position on the organization's plans and priorities, as you customarily would in the ideal bureaucracy. Instead, customize a position that, above all, reflects Dead Wood's unique, individual needs and personal interests. Everyone has a skill-set that can be exploited. If Dead Wood's skills and talents do not measure up to the level of his job description, then revise his job description downward. If his abilities don't reach the demands of his position, then adapt Dead Wood's position. If Dead Wood cannot do his job, then make the job fit what he can do. Don't fire the person, fix the position! Stop looking at Dead Wood only through the lens of his job description and assigned work role. Put yourself in his feet and see the organization through his eyes. You already know the best interests of the company. Get to know Dead Wood's personal professional tastes and preferences. Then give him a job to do that conforms. Play up Dead Wood's know-how, no matter how little he knows. Put Dead Wood in charge of the department's coffee machine, reordering clerical supplies, maintaining attendance records, disbursing petty cash, and purchasing postage stamps. Every department would welcome its own private travel agent, party planner, and cheerleader. There are plenty of odd jobs and busywork that need to be done even as they fall between the cracks because they are never assigned to anyone. Nonessential does not mean unnecessary. The right stuff is in the eye of the beholder. Instead of urging Dead Wood to tackle grand, lofty objectives, concentrate on smaller or more focused tasks. Doing so – nothing is too small and nothing is too insignificant to belong in Dead Wood's job description – can pay off in unexpected ways with unanticipated benefits. Dirty work that fits Dead Wood's skills and interests, yielding a strong sense of accomplishment and belonging, can turn Dead Wood into useful Fire Wood. How many inept airline pilots are there, that are potentially gifted copilots, but are screwing-up decision after decision because they are involved over their heads? Wouldn't it make more sense to redefine their role from decision-making to listening, taking notes, and reporting? Bring Dead Wood's work role into conformity with Dead Wood's talents and preferences. Then, where you lead, Dead Wood will follow – not because of your position power, but because they consider it to be in their own selfish interests to comply. At the risk of repeating myself, let me repeat myself: Put the cart before the horse that walks backward.

III. Thou shalt spoil efficiency to spare effectiveness.

The twin pillars of organizational productivity are Efficiency and Effectiveness. Efficiency essentially refers to accomplishing a task or goal by expending the least possible amount of time and attention. Effectiveness means how well or completely done a job is, no matter how long and how much energy it takes. And as a society, for better or worse, when we are required to choose between a job well done and a job done quickly, Efficiency is paramount. Contemporary American culture dictates that at every moment, society must be ultra conscious of using time, and obsessively committed to saving time and maximizing efficiency. In the modern working world, the pursuit of time saving and labor saving go hand in hand, to shape organizational behavior and drive organizational change. To paraphrase Gandhi, there is nothing more important to our way of life than increasing its speed. On the other hand, Dead Wood has a knack for concocting the most inventive ways of wasting company time, and for producing on demand the most plausible excuses for being behind schedule and missing deadlines than there are ticks on a monkey. In a nutshell, Dead Wood never faces a deadline that cannot be ignored and always needs extra time to get his work done. To borrow Parkinson's phrase, "Time available expands to put off the work from its completion." Stop expecting efficiency from Dead Wood! Focus *only* on his effectiveness. Is Dead Wood moving forward and following through, albeit at a snail's pace? Is Dead Wood doing a good job so far? Don't bother setting artificial deadlines and establishing timetables. These are utterly useless as motivational devices. "Yesterday today was tomorrow. Tomorrow today will be yesterday." Yesterday, today, tomorrow – Dead Wood cannot appreciate any difference between them. Learn to think as those around you think: Yesterday's work will be finished today as soon as it is tomorrow. The clock does not know whether it is early or late, and neither does Dead Wood. So pay no attention to his inefficiencies. Assign work to Dead Wood that is not time-bound, emphasize progress, and then learn to be satisfied with effective completion. In every work group, there are plenty of serious jobs that need to be completed regardless of what the clock says. Jobs that must be done well, not necessarily in a hurry. So, it won't much matter when Dead Wood is through, as long as he is finished. Sooner is always better than later, but Done is best. Consider the alternative, meaning, to compromise Dead Wood's effectiveness in order to gain more precious efficiency. Sure, Dead Wood would get the job done quickly, but so poorly that it would not be worth doing in the first place. The price of turning useless Dead Wood into useful Fire Wood may be to sacrifice efficiency to save effectiveness.

IV. Thou shalt snatch the pebble of success from the hand of failure.

All organizations and their members commit two kinds of mistakes. Let's call them Type I and Type II. Type I mistakes occur when organizations fail to do something that should have been done. And Type II mistakes occur when organizations do something that should never have been done. Cigarette manufacturers should have warned their customers that smoking causes cancer when they first discovered it. That was a Type I mistake that led to a Type II mistake, namely, the cover-up. And the Coca-Cola Company should never have replaced Classic Coke with New Coke, perhaps the greatest Type II blunder in corporate history. Dead Wood, being the classic underachiever, is usually associated with poor work habits, low energy, weak commitment, sloppy execution and leisurely follow-through. Consequently, Dead Wood is blamed a lot more often for making the first type of mistake. That is to say, Dead Wood does not finish a job that needed doing, and as a result, the organization suffered. However, bear with me. If Dead Wood does not complete a job that should *not* be done, then Dead Wood's failure to follow through to successful completion may be seen as an asset rather than a liability. If the job is worthwhile and important, and success is necessary for the organization to receive a benefit or gain an advantage, then the job may be right for the organization, but considering his deficiencies and weaknesses, Dead Wood becomes the wrong person to do it. Conversely, if the job is going to turn out badly, and success means that the organization will be hurt, then the organization is better off if the job is never finished, making Dead Wood the right person to do it. Whether or not the job he is given deserves to be successfully completed because of its positive or negative end product or final results is the key to turning Dead Wood to one's advantage. That sort of crystal-balling is easier to do than it sounds. Do you remember the last time your boss asked you to work on a project that you "know" is a waste of time? Do you remember those plans you submitted for innovations that you "know" will never be implemented? Do you remember the recommendations you made that you "know" have no chance of approval? Do you remember all the other foolish assignments you worked so hard on that you "know" are a dead-end street? Be honest. There are always plenty of Type II jobs in the pipeline waiting to be done. You don't have to be told which jobs lead nowhere. They don't need to be flagged. You just "know" them when you see them. Look at these jobs as opportunities to leverage Dead Wood's weaknesses. There are even plenty of jobs that ought to be screwed up, simply because they are detrimental to the organization and not worth doing to begin with. Ask the impossible of anyone, and he is bound to fail. Ask the impossible (or a lot less) of Dead Wood, and if the organization is better off without it, then when Dead Wood fails, consider it a job well done. Everyone accepts that some assignments are more important and add more value than others in the company. It follows that the least of assignments either will be so worthless in their accomplishment that they are a waste of time, or so damaging in their achievement that if they have to get started, then they shouldn't be completed. Learn to use your bureaucratic instincts to separate the sheep from the goats, and there can be no success sweeter than Dead Wood's failures.

𝔙. 𝔗𝔥𝔬𝔲 𝔰𝔥𝔞𝔩𝔱 𝔪𝔢𝔞𝔫 𝔪𝔢𝔞𝔫𝔰 𝔞𝔫𝔡 𝔪𝔢𝔞𝔫 𝔢𝔫𝔡𝔰.

Dead Wood loves to meet. Dead Wood loves to plan. Dead Wood loves to discuss. Today's work organization, more than ever, is an assembly of strangers from across oceans and cultures, a fitting together of disparate personalities to make a whole. Committees, teams, and work groups of all sizes and shapes are where the organization obliterates individuality in order to build community, and casts aside the illusion of psychology for the only true reality, sociology. The post-modern answer to the pre-modern question of why do people behave as they do no longer centers on the human personality with its inner drives and motives. Personality is out. The social relationship is in. Teamwork and the committee meeting has become one of the defining, essential characteristics of the 21st Century working world. To enter the world, every idea must go through an individual. To enter today's corporate world, every decision must go through a committee. That's why committees and committee meetings are as common as stink on a monkey. But committee meetings are only a means to an end. That is to say, the basic purpose of a committee meeting is for the group to determine the work that needs to be done, and decide who needs to be doing it. Think about it. Nothing else is really accomplished at the meeting itself. The meeting is a tool used to define and delegate work that then needs accomplishing elsewhere in the workplace, such as an assembly line, operating room, or classroom. Dead

Wood, however, tends to use committee meetings of every kind not as a means to achieving a goal, but as a goal in itself. Let's imagine Dead Wood is put in charge of a committee to develop a plan to implement Project X. Today, the committee is meeting for the twelfth time to touch up its plan for Project X. The good news is that the plan has remained essentially unchanged for the last ten meetings. The bad news is that Dead Wood opens the meeting by asking everyone to introduce himself, and then asks if the same time and place is okay with everyone else for next month's meeting. For Dead Wood, meeting is enough. That *is* the accomplishment. Meeting is an end in itself. To paraphrase Woody Allen, 99 44/100 percent of Dead Wood's working life consists of showing up. Even after he manages to turn showing up into a job description, Dead Wood continues to disrespect the means-end relationship. Suppose you and your fellow committee members decide to continue working on Project X over lunch today. Dead Wood will assume Patton-like command, survey what each person usually eats and drinks, microscopically research and select a restaurant, and pre-order food from the menu before arriving. The last time you saw Dead Wood that energized about something, it was a new floating holiday. In the end, Dead Wood will devote many more times the attention to planning lunch than he ever will to planning Project X. Planning requires execution to turn goals into accomplishments. And execution means treating means as means and ends as ends and always being aware of the difference. Changing Dead Wood into Fire Wood often begins when Dead Wood stops taking his eyes off the ball and stops seeing means as ends in themselves. As manager or workmate of Dead Wood, you will see a great deal of smoke but little fire. You will see a great deal of busyness but little to show for it. That can mean Dead Wood has drifted into confusing his goals with the means intended to achieve them. Drift Wood!? You will need to add clarity until Dead Wood is able to distinguish between them again, and progress. "Part the clouds, and reveal the true sky." When Dead Wood understands the difference between results and Results, then you will know he has turned a corner. In changing Dead Wood's busyness into Fire Wood's productivity, means mean means and ends mean ends.

Ⅵ. Thou shalt pound sand.

Compared to teammates, peers, and co-workers, management has a lot more at risk and considerably more to lose from its relationship with Dead Wood. First, you, being management, have only so much that you can do about Dead Wood. On the options scale, yours range from 9 to 10 – 10 meaning Totally Ineffective. Second, the most promising solution and the best you can do may very well be to back away, keep your hands off, and let the situation take its course. Here is your predicament. You know that you have Dead Wood. Your boss knows that you have Dead Wood. Your peers know that you have Dead Wood. Your subordinates know that you have Dead Wood. And Dead Wood knows that he is underperforming and not doing his job. Even Dead Wood knows that he is Dead Wood. And all of them, Dead Wood included, are expecting you to do something meaningful. Fear not! Let's go through your two options. If you fail to act, then everyone else will conclude that you are weak and stupid. Throughout the organization, your colleagues will lose much of their respect for you, and when one of them speaks your name, the rest will shake their heads and stare at the floor. To boot, once people make up their minds about what kind of person you are, it is not impossible to change them. But the change is always from a good impression to a bad one. The damage to your public image and professional reputation won't matter only if the next step on your career path is the priesthood. Dead Wood will interpret your Star Trek-like noninterference directive as a sign of weakness, which it just might be. If you think that up to now Dead Wood has been difficult to manage and engage and has taken too many liberties, then look out, Dr. Frankenstein, the monster is loose! Dead Wood will cause more mischief under a weak supervisor than under no management authority at all. Would Satan hector the living as much if he weren't competing with God? Do I have to draw you a picture? Okay, you have one and only one option. You *must* respond to Dead Wood with action, not reflection. The good news is that your efforts will enhance your standing in the organization and gain great face with your colleagues. The better news is that will happen no matter how successful or unsuccessful your efforts prove to be. Because everyone knows that Dead Wood is an abstruse, intractable problem and an insurmountable challenge, no one seriously expects you to succeed. In fact, it may be more advantageous to you *not* to succeed inasmuch as unsuccessful efforts earn both admiration *and* sympathy. Try and fail. It's a win-win!

VII. Thou shalt curse thy neighbor's house as thy neighbor has cursed yours.

Do any of these urban myths sound familiar? Purely as a result of a series of accidental fortunate discoveries, a hospital physician is caught poisoning to death his otherwise healthy patients because, as Dr. Death calmly explains to the authorities, he was ordered to kill them by the Angel of the Bottomless Pit, known to the rest of us as his next-door neighbor's pet bulldog who goes by the name of Sparky. In popular culture, different characters tend to populate this same story. A stockbroker with a drug habit steals from his investors. A pharmacist with a gambling habit deals drugs. An airline pilot with a drinking problem falls asleep at the wheel. These are the worst kind of myths, *true* myths. And all of them have the same unhappy ending. The police invariably find that the culprit (a) carried out his heinous crimes under the very noses of his clueless peers and co-workers who should have been the first to suspect that something fishy was going on, and (b) was trusted with a position of great responsibility and authority because he presented impeccable recommendations from his previous employer and glowing testimonials from his former colleagues who still can't believe *that* was the weird smell coming from his office. In literally every occupation and profession, there is Dead Wood. And where there is Dead Wood, there will be a cover-up. Ironically, in the classic life-and-death professions – medicine, law, and the clergy – that are empowered by society to be self-governing and therefore are required to be self-correcting to protect us from them, Dead Wood is often passed around from one institution, firm, or parish to another, building a reputation that grows more impressive with every washout. This is one of the evil humours that has infected modern medicine for years. Physicians with dubious work histories move from hospital to hospital, able to keep their incompetencies hidden from their patients because colleagues and past employers refuse to share all that they know. And Dead Wood's blunders are likely to become increasingly desperate and offensive when he is on the verge of being caught, which tends to accelerate re-employment. Therefore, salesmanship may be the answer for you, too. In other words, market Dead Wood as Fire Wood, and market your problem as the next employer's solution. If you want to get rid of Dead Wood, stop seeing him as your adversary, and start seeing yourself as his advocate. The day after his Farewell Party, *replace* Dead Wood with Fire Wood. It happens all the time, and it works. Why? Because of The Toilet Assumption: Once it is flushed down the drain, you don't have to worry about it anymore, because it no longer exists. The biggest challenge you will face when applying this particular strategy will be how to square it with your awareness of right and wrong, and your compulsion to do right. I won't sugarcoat it: You do not want this commandment to become a kind of universal law, and for everyone else to act according to the same principle. Be honest: You want to dump your trash on your neighbor's lawn, but you expect your neighbor to keep his troubles in his own house, and far away from yours. On the other hand, there is a high probability that's how you were stuck with Dead Wood in the first place. Your predecessor screwed you, so, technically, treating the next employer the same way may not be altogether wrong. Second, everyone deserves a second chance, Dead Wood included. Third, if you can get rid of Dead Wood, regardless of how underhandedly, and you choose not to, then you may be guilty of professional negligence, which is the greater fault. Finally, your feelings of self-reproach, from believing that you have done a wrong, will pass quickly, to be replaced by a lightness of being that only the once heavy laden can understand.

VIII. Thou shalt pour old wine into new wineskins.

Some women have a way of turning men into boys,
and others of turning boys into men. The working
world also has a way of turning useful Fire Wood
into useless Dead Wood, and turning some Dead
Wood into Fire Wood. As of this writing, the nation
is fighting two wars in the Middle East, and the U.S.
Army is having a great deal of difficulty enlisting new
foot soldiers to fill its depleted ranks. So the Army has
been saturating this summer's television programming
with a brand-new advertising campaign designed to
attract new recruits. What is unusual about these new
TV commercials is that their message is not aimed at
twenty-somethings, but at their moms and dads. Does
your son or daughter have an immature resistance to
authority? Is he or she disrespectful, lazy, or foolish?
Does he play all the time and refuse to live his life
in quiet desperation like the rest of us? Does he
behave unthinkingly and unreflectingly, and then deny
responsibility for his mistakes? Perfect! Because the
military stands ready to transform him into a mature,
solid, hard working, courageous warrior you can be
justly proud of. How? By arming him, by putting
him in harm's way, by trusting him to defend and
protect his country against all enemies, by giving him
command of your neighbor's sons and daughters on
the battlefield, and by placing billions of dollars worth
of high-tech weapons of mass destruction under his
control. In a word, this is known as Empowerment.
And empowerment works. It works by motivating the

individual to identify his personal goals with the goals of the group until there is a complete coincidence of the Me and the We. Remember St. Paul on the road to Damascus before and after his epiphany. It may seem like a crazy and counter-intuitive thing to do, but empowering can bring out the best in Dead Wood, and what he can be, he becomes. A touch of authority and responsibility, a little demonstration of trust and confidence, can work miracles on Dead Wood's attitude and job performance. St. Paul, once one of the greatest persecutors of early Christians, became one of Christianity's greatest apostles. By no means is human nature immutable, Dead Wood included. If he cannot follow orders, then empower him to give orders. If others cannot depend on him, then make him dependent on them. If he cannot follow, then appoint him to lead. Mediocre followership is often a symptom of latent leadership. Custer, Grant, and Patton were all routinely insubordinate. Turn the tables on Dead Wood, and watch him rise to the challenge! You will find that a little power will go to one's head, and the one who used to ask what the company can do for him, is now the one asking what others can do for the company.

IX. Thou shalt first know thyself.

Use your sociological imagination for a moment: An airplane crash-lands in the Sahara and there are two survivors. They are stranded in the desert with one and only one water supply between them, a small canteen. Suppose one of the survivors sees the canteen as being half-filled. While the other survivor sees the same canteen as half-empty. Which survivor is right? What do you think? Is the canteen half-filled or half-empty? You may choose to take the position that it doesn't make any difference what one believes. A canteen is a canteen is a canteen. The canteen is what it is, period. But then you would be altogether wrong. For whether one believes that the canteen is half-filled or is half-empty matters a great deal. Here's why. Which of the survivors is more likely to be the first one to drink from the canteen? Will it be the survivor who believes that the canteen is more filled, or the other one who believes that it is more empty? Obviously, the right answer is that the survivor who believes that the canteen is half-filled is more likely to drink first. And the survivor who believes that the canteen is half-empty is more likely to hold back and refrain from drinking. That's because our beliefs come true when we behave as if they are true. So if the survivor who believes that the canteen is half-filled behaves as if it is true by drinking first, then it is half-filled, but only for that survivor. And if the survivor who believes that the canteen is half-empty behaves according to his belief by holding back, then it is half-empty, but only for him. The truth is that the canteen is *both* half-filled and half-empty. For truth is not something outside your head just laying around waiting to be picked up and discovered. Truth is not a fishbowl that is the same for all the goldfish swimming in it. Truth is not a one-way street allowing everyone to move in one direction only. Truth is in the eye of the beholder.

What do you see? Half-filled Fire Wood or half-empty Dead Wood? You assume that everyone else sees other people just as you do. But the truth is, some do, some don't. One person's Dead Wood may be another person's Fire Wood. You look at a co-worker and see Dead Wood, and you think, he is "inexperienced." Your colleague looks at the same person in the same job and sees Fire Wood, and he thinks, that worker has "potential." Dead Wood is "slow." But Fire Wood is "careful." Dead Wood is "stubborn and hard to handle." But Fire Wood is "independent." Labels matter. They operate like inner gyroscopes, guiding our actions, beliefs, and emotions. Turning useless Dead Wood into useful Fire Wood may need to begin with you examining critically your own taken-for-granted beliefs and assumptions, and losing your illusions. All of us have seen an enemy only to realize later on that we may have found a friend had we not let our illusions get the better of us. In today's top-down, chain of command-driven workplace, it is easy to confuse the behavioral richness and diversity of those around us with nonconformity. Instead of using our creativity and imagination to find ways to put those differences to work for us, we make ourselves miserable struggling in vain to dress everyone in the same straitjacket that we have put on our view of the working world.

Dead Wood sees itself as adding "special" value to the organization and, therefore, is not subject to standard operating rules and ordinary expectations. It is pointless to order them to do anything. Instead, Dead Wood should be seen as a volunteer work force. And management should see itself less like military commanders and more like gameshow hosts. It's never too late to discover Fire Wood where you once found only Dead Wood. It all depends on changing your perspective and point of view and seeing those around you through different lenses. Who once described insanity as behaving the same way but expecting a different result? "You must be the change you wish to see in the world," in the words of Mohandas Gandhi. The perfect workplace you desire is not here or there. It cannot be seen or touched. If you look for it, you will not find it. For it lies within you!

Survival Norm #24: Learn to Recognize Success

Fear is the new fuel of the American worker. Fear of success. Fear of failure. Fear of flying too high, rising too fast, and drowning in unfulfilled expectations. Fear of flying too low, missing opportunities, and drowning in unfulfilled aspirations. Fear of working too hard and collapsing miserable and alone. Fear of not working hard enough and starving miserable and alone. But you can't go around afraid of everything. No matter how much you worry and how careful you are, hits happen. You succeed. You fail. Fear not! It's never, ever the end of the world. No question, some self-appointed management gurus preach that fixing Dead Wood's weaknesses is a foolish waste of time. That it's the rare employee who can be motivated to change his work habits from Dead Wood to Fire Wood, even when the personal rewards are obvious and substantial. Bullhits! Every one of us knows people who went from lukewarm to burning hot, from a marriage of convenience to falling madly in love with their work, from quiet desperation to pouring their heart and soul into their job, and from good to great. Indifference can indeed be the father of enthusiasm … if you know how. In the end, your relationship with Dead Wood will have run its course when you have achieved what you sought, and success means, essentially, right-behavior. It's a triune structure consisting of right-actions, right-ideas, and right-attitudes. What do you want him to do? Why do you want him to do it? What do you want him to feel is in it for him? That's total success! You can't get there from here without negotiating with Dead Wood, and understanding what makes him tick makes all the difference in bargaining. First, Dead Wood will never say yes to your first offer. That would admit weakness and show submission. So don't blow your stack on the first hand. Second, what you're asking Dead Wood to give up is a hundred times more important to him than you think it is. So don't miscalculate his emotional attachment. Third, whatever you think will lower Dead Wood's resistance to saying yes will in fact increase it. So don't miscalculate your offer. You win when Dead Wood buys-in to right-actions and does what you want him to do. You also win when Dead Wood buys-in to your reasons, purpose, and vision. And you win again when Dead Wood buys-in to how everyone will benefit if the team scores. Learn to recognize success! It's not an all or nothing game. Like a prizefight, measure winning in rounds.

X. Thou shalt be cool.

Nowadays, everywhere you turn, machines are winning the race with humans, forcing people to confront their limitations. Computers are now capable of playing chess better than any human can. A clever, over-the-counter software routine can now design a building, prepare a tax return, or buy and sell stock better and faster than an architect, accountant, or stockbroker. Sweeping across the retail world today, computers, programmed to deliver an impressive range of consumer services, are proving to have more effective people skills, to build stronger relationships with customers, and to have a better overall rapport with humans than human providers do. Automobiles have been able to "run" faster than any human being has for almost a century. In short, machine technology is increasingly becoming more human than human.

Over the horizon, there must be a limit to how fast the human body can run a mile, how high a person can jump, and how long a human being under water can hold one's breath, and it's only a matter of time before we achieve all of these limits. When that happens, it will nevertheless change nothing. People will never stop competing in these sports along with other contests of skill and endurance for the very same reason that we have not already given up practicing chess or studying architecture.

That's because of what really drives us to work and play harder and strive to become better and greater in the first place.

As much as we like in popular culture to uncomplicate the working world by comparing it to an arena where athletes go to compete against each other for scarce and valued resources, that's not what motivates most people to go to work, and that doesn't help explain why they behave as they do in the workplace. Athletes do not train and sacrifice simply to be able to outplay their opponent. And workers do not dedicate themselves to work longer, better, and faster simply to outperform their peers, human or machine. That's not what marketing gurus mean by the catchy slogan, "Be all that you can be." If that were true, once an athlete discovered an opponent that he could not hope to defeat, or a worker or owner discovered a rival or competitor he could not best, then they would no longer have any reason to try to win or even to try very hard. But losers are not quitters. Middle managers looking for the Glass Escalator don't quit when they hit the Glass Ceiling. The Boston Red Sox didn't quit, and the Chicago Cubs won't quit. The pursuit of excellence must be motivated by something more than malicious or smug Schadenfreude taken in Dead Wood's incompetence or somebody else's disappointment. Otherwise, computer technology, not to mention his betters, would have easily crushed Fire Wood's will to power long ago.

Winning is not the only thing after all. We do not excel simply to surpass our peers, mankind or man-made.

By conducting a revealing thought-experiment, let's explore the other side of the same coin, that is the drive to attain absolute limits of human endurance and performance. In an imaginary future, scientists dealing with the vital processes and physiology of the human body make a disturbing claim. They discover that the human skeleton in peak conditioning can never run a mile faster than three minutes flat. Now suppose, in future-world, there already are ten athletes who have run the three-minute-mile. Will they choose to continue their training? Will they decide to give up racing forever, and find a new sport? After all, in a contest with all of the runners racing at their best, the only outcome that any one can hope for is a ten-way tie. What motivated them to start training in the first place? Was it just to achieve the absolute fastest humanly possible speed?

No.

In one all-important respect, Dead Wood and Fire Wood are the same kind of person. They work, but not to feel superior, and not to reach for and grasp any absolutes of human achievement. Fire Wood may work harder and better than Dead Wood. But both Fire Wood and Dead Wood use the working world like a tool to achieve the dreams they have about themselves. The work experience is used to achieve an image of the person one desires to be as opposed to the person one actually is. The crucial difference between Fire Wood and Dead Wood is that for Fire Wood, the person he wants to be and the person the organization feels he ought to be are one and the same person.

One powerful technique for turning useless Dead Wood into useful Fire Wood is to steer Dead Wood's ideal conception of himself deliberately and carefully toward an image of the person that the organization wants, needs, and pays him to be.

How?

You are what you eat. Dead Wood will behave more like Fire Wood when Dead Wood possesses an excess of attitudes and beliefs favorable to organizational success as opposed to attitudes and beliefs unfavorable to organizational success.

How?

No one is born human. Human behavior is learned behavior. And people covet what they see. Therefore, by working closely with Fire Wood as role model, cheerleader, and coach, Dead Wood will observe, internalize, and reflect favorable attitudes and behavior patterns, gradually extinguishing the unfavorable ones. "Existence precedes essence." Psychology recapitulates sociology.

The more popular and common sense approach is to keep Dead Wood away from Fire Wood, and the more segregated the two worlds, the better. Dead Wood contributes little to organizational success, and Fire Wood, lots. "It only takes one rotten apple to spoil a whole barrel." Leave the Dead Wood to bury the Dead Wood. Wrong. The problem with that solution is when the blind lead the blind, they both walk off a cliff. Likes attract, and worse. They form alliances and networks that reinforce bad behavior and make even the right solutions more difficult to apply and more uncertain to succeed. Former POTUS LBJ, speaking of his political adversaries, said, "I'd rather have them inside my tent pissing out than outside pissing in." Don Corleone put it differently, "Keep your friends close, but your enemies closer." Wrong behavior begets wrong behavior. Right behavior begets right behavior.

If you want Dead Wood to become more like Fire Wood, then you must put them on the same team, make them work together, and reinforce their working relationship. Parenting Dead Wood to help him live up to your expectations, or at least his job description, is a job for Fire Wood. People anxiously look to others for approval and we will do almost anything to be popular and fit in. Peer pressure, in an other-directed society like ours, is simply irresistible. Fire Wood can influence Dead Wood to try on a different self, almost like new clothing, and following from this, engage in different, more productive right-stuff behavior. That is the one pivotal truth you must take away from everything else we have discussed and on which hangs everything else you have learned. The outer world of things, people, and events shapes the inner world of meaning, feeling, and emotion. "The structures of society become the structures of our own consciousness." That governing dynamic should be the single most important and effective tool in your attitude and behavior modification workshop. Keep your cool. Pick your fights. But learn the art of fighting without fighting. Don't make threats. But don't ever walk away from one. And, above all, be believing that everything, always, is transpiring as it should. The American philosopher William James wrote, "Act for the best, hope for the best, and take what comes." In other words, be cool.

Survival Norm #25: The Greatest Enemy of Choosing is Choice

Choice is not always a good idea. Most people do not know how to choose properly or they simply refuse to choose because having many choices, or lack of choice, can be inhibiting. When the choices are complex, the options are too many or too few, and the stakes are high, people are easily paralyzed into making the worst of all possible decisions – to do nothing. Is this the reason why so many top leaders and decision-makers in Corporate America have a Magic 8-Ball, the small, plastic fortune-telling toy, on their desks? Do they need help making choices? "Signs point to yes." Now that you've almost finished reading this book, you can't possibly try everything you've learned. And not every idea deserves equal billing. So, with too many new ideas about how to handle Dead Wood, you need to separate the ideas that will work for you from the real stinkers. Are you ready to choose? Let's begin by setting some boundaries to choice. First, decide what you want to accomplish. What is your desired objective in dealing with Dead Wood? Be selective. Is it to marginalize, socialize, compartmentalize, demonize, tranquilize, energize, or minimize Dead Wood? Pick one at a time. Start with the goal that will yield the greatest good for the greatest number of people. This is all-important because solutions derive from preferences. Second, if you have the smallest doubt about a strategy or planned course of action, then reject it. Because if you have faith and do not waver, and believe in your heart that you have chosen wisely, then you have. Focus on a limited number of solutions. Sometimes, touchdowns are just not possible on every play. Be satisfied with a first down. Boxers know that a fight is rounds. Third, map your preferences onto your solutions. Your preferences should give rise to appropriate solutions, and your solutions should achieve your preferences. Adjust right-thinking and right-effort to fit. There should be no wasted motion or wasted attention. Finally, start with the most important results and solutions and work forward from theory to action. Now that you understand what has to be done, and why, you will always be clear and make the right choices.

Thirteen:
Forest for the Trees:

Work is not slavery or captivity. Work is not the enemy of freedom. Work *is* freedom. Work is the source and an infinite ocean of dignity and self-worth. Pleasure, Wealth, Fame, Power – work is the key to every lock in the material world. Freud wrote in "Civilization and Its Discontents" that nothing anchors a person in the real-life, flesh-and-blood world like work. Work gives life meaning.

The greatest mistake that you can make is jumping to the conclusion that Dead Wood does not feel the same about work as you do. That's a popular theory, but that's not the problem. Dead Wood wants to earn the very same "psychic income" from work as you do. If it were the problem, then your situation would be hopeless because, again, according to Freud and most of the science of modern sociology, not long after we climb down from mother's lap, our deepest beliefs and core personal values have crystallized, and for the most part are irreversible. So there is reason for optimism.

Program yourself to think of the workplace as a marriage in which your spouse or partner is your job, and your colleagues and co-workers are your in-laws. You choose your job, but you cannot choose your colleagues. Neither can you choose how or why they behave as they do. Dead Wood may be a problem in your company. It may be a serious problem. But it's not just your problem, and it's not your only problem. The ancient Chinese put it this way, "A job is half a life." So be gentle with yourself. Strive to be happy.

Success in turning your don't-go-to, useless Dead Wood into useful Fire Wood, and finding peace of mind and contentment, begins with a clear understanding of one principle: Some things are within your control, and some things are not. I have showed you some of the things you *can* change. Trying to control or to change what you can't only results in frustration and disappointment. If anything is outside your control, then discipline yourself to see it as someone else's business, and none of yours. Don't worry about it. First, learn to distinguish between what you can and cannot change. Then, keep your efforts focused like a laser beam on what you can freely and effectively change and improve. Don't waste your time and effort wrestling with things that are beyond your control. Change what you can. Leave the rest to others. Long story short, you must become part St. Francis, part Thomas Edison, and part General Patton.

I have tried to help you discover what you should do. That's the easy part. You will always know what not to do. The hard part is not doing it.

Take courage, knowing that you are going to make mistakes, lots of them. But keep trying, knowing that risk-taking may be the first step toward failure, but success is also impossible without it.

Robert M. Khoury, Ph.D.
New York   Georgia   Florida